DATE DUE			

5/96

THEotherAMERICA

The HOMELESS

by
Gail B. Stewart

Lucent Books, P.O. Box 289011, San Diego, CA 92198-9011

These and other titles are included in *The Other America* series:

The Elderly

People with AIDS

Teenage Mothers

Library of Congress Cataloging-in-Publication Data
Stewart, Gail, 1949-
     The homeless / by Gail B. Stewart
         p. cm.—(The other America)
     Includes bibliographical references (p. 109) and index.
     ISBN 1-56006-331-9 (alk. paper)
     1. Homeless persons—United States—Interviews—Juvenile literature.
[1. Homeless persons—United States—Interviews. 2. Homelessness.]
I.Title. II. Series: Stewart, Gail, 1949– Other America.
HV4505.S75   1996
305.5'.36—dc20   95-40336
[B]   CIP
                                                                          AC

Printed in the U.S.A.
Copyright © 1996 by Lucent Books, Inc.
P.O. Box 289011, San Diego, CA 92198-9011

Contents

FOREWORD 4

INTRODUCTION 6

MARILYN 11
In her early fifties, Marilyn has moved in and out of homelessness several times. Marilyn's abusive marriages and difficult relationship with her daughter have brought her to a life on the streets.

BEN AND ANN 33
In their early thirties, Ben and Ann found themselves suddenly homeless, living in a shelter with their three children. Far from their extended families, Ben and Ann must try to get together enough funds to rent another home.

TRINA 57
Having just given birth to her sixth child, twenty-two-year-old Trina lives on the streets and in shelters, attempting to keep body and soul together. Trina's family has never known a stable home.

ARNOLDO 78
A political refugee from Guatemala, Arnoldo's expired work permit leaves him unable to work legally and attain enough money to escape homelessness. Far from bleak, Arnoldo's street life is filled with constructive activities.

EPILOGUE 106

WAYS YOU CAN GET INVOLVED 107

FOR FURTHER READING 109

INDEX 110

ABOUT THE AUTHOR 112

Foreword

O, YES,
I SAY IT PLAIN,
AMERICA NEVER WAS AMERICA TO ME.
AND YET I SWEAR THIS OATH—
AMERICA WILL BE!
LANGSTON HUGHES

Perhaps more than any other nation in the world, the United States represents an ideal to many people. The ideal of equality— of opportunity, of legal rights, of protection against discrimination and oppression. To a certain extent, this image has proven accurate. But beneath this ideal lies a less idealistic fact—many segments of our society do not feel included in this vision of America.

They are the outsiders—the homeless, the elderly, people with AIDS, teenage mothers, gang members, prisoners, and countless others. When politicians and the media discuss society's ills, the members of these groups are defined as what's wrong with America; they are the people who need fixing, who need help, or increasingly, who need to take more responsibility. And as these people become society's fix-it problem, they lose all identity as individuals and become part of an anonymous group. In the media and in our minds these groups are identified by condition—a disease, crime, morality, poverty. Their condition becomes their identity, and once this occurs, in the eyes of society, they lose their humanity.

The Other America series reveals the members of these groups as individuals. Through in-depth interviews, each person tells his or her unique story. At times these stories are painful, revealing individuals who are struggling to maintain their integrity, their humanity, their lives, in the face of fear, loss, and economic and spiritual hardship. At other times, their tales are exasperating, demonstrating a litany of poor choices, shortsighted thinking, and self-gratification. Nevertheless, their identities remain distinct, their personalities diverse.

As we listen to the people of *The Other America* series describe their experiences they cease to be stereotypically defined and become tangible, individual. In the process, we may begin to understand more profoundly and think more critically about society's problems. When politicians debate, for example, whether the homeless problem is due to a poor economy or lack of initiative, it will help to read the words of the homeless. Perhaps then we can see the issue more clearly. The family who finds itself temporarily homeless because it has always been one paycheck from poverty is not the same as the mother of six who has been chronically chemically dependent. These people's circumstances are not all of one kind, and perhaps we, after all, are not so very different from them. Before we can act to solve the problems of the Other America, we must be willing to look down their path, to see their faces. And perhaps in doing so, we may find a piece of ourselves as well.

Introduction

WHO ARE THE HOMELESS?

They are in every city in America. Some are almost stereotypes—down-and-out men huddling on park benches or rummaging through garbage cans, an old woman talking to herself as she pushes a cart filled with an odd mix of possessions down a city street. These street people are the most visible of the homeless. However, the homeless are a much more varied group.

"For every wino lounging on a park bench or passed out in a doorway, I can name you six or seven who aren't," says one advocate for the homeless. "I can show you women who are homeless because of getting beat up by their boyfriends. I can show you people who can't find housing because it's too expensive, or it's in short supply. I also can show you little kids that haven't got a clue why they're home one minute and crammed into some lousy shelter the next.

"People think it's all about bums, all about drunks. And, hey—I'd be lying if I told you that chemical abuse doesn't play a big role in some of these people's situations. But if you're looking for an easy answer, I got news for you—there ain't none. If you want to blame people, we can start looking in the mirror, blaming ourselves for not doing anything about homelessness a long time ago, for letting the problem get as big as it is today."

HOW MANY?

Just how big is the population of homeless people in the United States today? It depends, say experts, both on who is doing the counting, and who is being counted.

For example, a well-known advocacy group called the National Coalition for the Homeless (NCH) estimated in the mid-1980s that the number of homeless people in the United States might be as high as 3 million. On the other hand, the U.S. Department of Housing and Urban Development (HUD) had much lower estimates: between 250,000 and 350,000.

Each organization questioned the other. HUD complained that the National Coalition for the Homeless was intentionally inflating its estimate to draw more attention to its cause, while the NCH accused HUD of using an incorrect definition of homelessness. The NCH said that the HUD survey only counted people who lived on the streets or in shelters. Those living in inadequate housing, such as tents, automobiles, or vacant buildings, were not counted. Nor were people living temporarily with friends or relatives.

But even using HUD's narrower definition of homelessness, writes sociologist Christopher Jencks in his book *The Homeless*, the number of people sleeping in public places or in shelters has increased fourfold in the past fifteen years. Who are the homeless, and why are their numbers increasing so dramatically?

A Change for the Worse

Homelessness is certainly not a new problem; America has always had its share of destitute people. As far back as the 1750s, reports of beggars and vagabonds wandering from village to village in search of a meal and a place to sleep were frequent. In the years immediately following the Civil War, drunken men sleeping in gutters were a common sight in major U.S. cities.

The Great Depression of the 1930s turned thousands of working men and women into homeless people, and special programs as part of President Franklin D. Roosevelt's New Deal were initiated to provide temporary housing for them. World Wars I and II provided some relief for the homeless problem, for the outbreak of war meant plenty of factory jobs for the poor.

Homeless vagrants commonly known as skid row bums were a fairly consistent problem after the end of World War II. Typically they were middle-aged men, unemployed and, usually, alcoholic. While a few slept on the streets, most spent their nights in what were known as single-room-occupancy (SRO) hotels. These were run down, infested with rats and cockroaches, but cheap—between thirty cents and fifty cents a night.

It was easy for most Americans to ignore these homeless people, for unless one walked through the poorest sections of the city, they were largely invisible. Being drunk in public or loitering in public places like bus stations and libraries was illegal, and police routinely rounded up offenders and took them to jail.

But the homeless of today are quite different. They are not a group comprised of middle-aged alcoholic men, and they are certainly not invisible. What has changed?

A New Kind of Homelessness

A number of factors have contributed to the makeup of the homeless population today. The large loss of well-paying jobs in manufacturing is a primary factor. Today it has been estimated that more than two million factory jobs—full-time, with benefits—have been erased each year since 1979. Instead of being replaced with full-time, well-paying jobs in other industries, the service industry has created a flood of jobs, usually minimum wage, with few if any benefits.

Another factor that has increased the population of the homeless is the closing of mental hospitals. Before the 1970s people judged by psychiatrists to be potentially dangerous to themselves or to society were placed in these institutions, often against their wills. In the 1970s, however, two changes occurred that resulted in hundreds of thousands of mentally ill people's being released from these institutions.

The first was a change in the laws. Many people, worried about the civil rights of the mentally ill, argued that it was wrong to put people in mental institutions just because someone thought they *might* be dangerous. Only those who have committed crimes, they argued, should be institutionalized.

The second was the invention of revolutionary new drugs that kept many mentally ill patients calmer. It was believed that if mentally ill people took their medications regularly, they could be released from the institutions. Instead of the large, state-run mental hospitals, communities would build smaller clinics to service the needs of their mentally ill patients, usually on an outpatient basis.

This optimistic scenario did not become reality. Whereas in the 1960s there were a half million beds available in public mental institutions, by 1980 there were fewer than one hundred thousand. To further complicate matters, the community mental-health clinics were not built in the numbers that had been promised.

When the state institutions released these patients with a week's supply of medication and a bag full of their clothing, many of them had nowhere to go. Many ended up in jails; many more who had no family to care for them ended up on the streets. And because so few community health centers were built, there were no supervisors to make sure those mentally ill people received and took their medications. The fallout of this decision is grim— almost one-third of the homeless in the United States are mentally ill and cannot care for themselves adequately.

CRACK AND HOMELESSNESS

Another variable that is part of the lives of many homeless people today is crack, a derivative of cocaine. Until the mid-1980s, when crack hit the streets, many of the homeless who were chemically dependent were alcoholics.

"A bottle of cheap wine could do the trick for those guys," says a thirty-year-old man named Mick, homeless for three years. "Cocaine was for rich people, so nobody on the streets used it. But when crack came along, that changed everything. It was lots cheaper than cocaine, so everybody could afford it. Nowadays for about four dollars you can get a hit of crack, and that will do everything liquor will do, and more. If you don't think crack is everywhere, you're dreaming. Every shelter I've ever been in, somebody's got some, somebody's selling."

The facts seem to bear this out. Urine samples taken from people in several New York shelters for men indicate that as many as 65 percent of the occupants had used the drug recently. The numbers for women are lower, but experts say that more and more homeless women, including those with young children, are using crack.

NO ONE CAUSE

People who work with the homeless say that scores of other reasons contribute to the changing, and expanding, population of homeless in the United States. Urban renewal, the effort to renovate the parts of town where the SRO hotels used to operate, have left many without shelter. Glittering new office buildings, parking ramps, and parks occupy the spaces where more than one million of those SRO's once were.

The rise in the cost of health care, the increase in the reported cases of wife- and child-battering, the rise in the numbers of illegal aliens, the millions of divorced women whose husbands neglect to pay their child support—all of these factors have combined to make today's homeless quite different from the homeless of twenty or thirty years ago.

This book, *The Other America: The Homeless*, tells four stories. Each is very different, as are the stories of any other four people in a large city. The only thing they share, in fact, is their lack of an address.

Marilyn is an Ojibwa, a Native American from a reservation in northern Minnesota. She has battled alcoholism and heroin addiction most of her adult life and now suffers from AIDS. Unable to get along with her adult daughter or to afford housing on her own, Marilyn lives in a shelter for women and families on the north side of Minneapolis.

Ben and Ann and their three children are a frightening reminder that not only the chemically dependent, the poverty stricken, or the mentally ill become homeless. His family became homeless, says Ben, "in the space of a few hours one night last spring." Unaware that a young man at their dinner table was wanted for murder, Ben and Ann and their children watched in horror as their house was destroyed by bullets and tear gas as the police captured the suspect. As the bureaucracy of the city drags slowly along, they wait for some reimbursement for the loss of their home and possessions.

Trina is a reminder, too—a reminder that it is usually not just one factor that leaves a person homeless. An astonishingly young mother of six, Trina has endured abuse from an alcoholic mother as well as a string of abusive boyfriends. Fighting a battle with crack addiction and alcoholism, she lives in a temporary shelter.

Finally, there is Arnoldo, a middle-aged man from Guatemala. He lives inside a bridge near the Mississippi and is very happy there. His life is a routine, but at least, he says, "I can stay out of the shelters, with all the crime and violence that are a big part of them."

The stories here are sometimes hopeful, often heartbreaking. As with others in marginal groups, some of the people here have made poor choices, others are victims of circumstance, and some are somewhere in between. A common fact about their lives, however, seems to be a warning for all of us: Without a constant vigilance over the choices we make, our lives can become nightmarishly unpredictable and purposeless.

Marilyn

"THAT'S THE STORY OF MY LIFE—
RUNNING, RUNNING, RUNNING.
ANY OLD PROBLEM, AND I RUN."

Although she is only in her early fifties, Marilyn calls herself "an elderly woman." She is Native American—Chippewa, she says, with the resigned look of one who is used to being misunderstood by others. When asked if Ojibwa was the preferred name of her heritage, she seems pleased, and nods. Marilyn is heavyset, her jet-black hair streaked with gray. She wears a bright pink, over-sized T-shirt, stained and torn. When she smiles, it is evident that she is missing a few teeth.

Marilyn has been homeless for a few months. She is currently staying at a shelter downtown, although she knows that her time limit there is only a month. After her month is up, she says, she isn't sure where she will go. Her health is bad, she says. Diagnosed with AIDS, Marilyn is facing not only the problem of homelessness, but the looming prospect of her own death.

"A SICK WAY OF LIFE"

Marilyn spent her childhood on the White Earth Reservation in northern Minnesota. It was then, she says with regret, that she started the cycle of running away that continued all her life.

"That was how I solved my problems," she says in a bitter voice. "I ran away from them. Every time things got bad, I ran. I wish now I hadn't done it; hopefully I've learned to stop that by now. But it started back in White Earth, many years ago.

"The reservation itself was not so bad," she shrugs. "We spent a lot of time playing in the woods, climbing trees, swimming in the lake. There was a lot of space there, lots more than in a city. It was just a different way of growing up, but it was not bad."

What *was* bad, Marilyn says quietly, was her family life on the reservation, a life that was filled with violence and abuse. It was a time that she cannot recall without a great deal of sadness, although it all happened more than forty years ago. When she talks about it, it is in a voice barely louder than a whisper, and tears sprinkle down onto the front of her shirt.

Marilyn says that she has been running all of her life, ever since she left the White Earth Reservation to escape an abusive father.

"My father was a strict man—way too strict," she explains. "He never gave in. He wouldn't allow us kids to talk to anyone outside of the family, wouldn't allow us even to talk at the table. That was hard being little, with so many rules that didn't make any sense. I used to think, boy, when I have kids of my own, there's no chance that I'll be that way to them, make them sit so quietly, so silent all the time. That isn't normal for kids.

"There were seven of us kids. Four were his; my three older brothers had a different father. A big family, but there was no joy there, no happiness. My father sort of led the way, being as mean as he was. As time went on, there was just anger in our family. Everyone fought, everyone screamed at everyone else. It was a sick way of life, a really sick way of life."

"IF I STAYED THERE, HE'D KILL ME"

Marilyn says that although everyone in the family fought, it was she who received the worst of her father's anger.

"He whipped me, he punched me, he threw things at me, he beat me up," she says, wiping tears away with a crumpled tissue. "I was the oldest of his kids. I had three older brothers, but they had a different father. I guess I took the punishment because I was the oldest of his kids, I don't know. My mother never really tried to get him to stop. Maybe she was afraid of him, too—I don't know.

"It got really bad when I got to the age where girls are noticing boys, and boys are noticing girls. He would say mean things about the way boys were with girls. It made it all seem really dirty. He told me I wasn't to go with no boys, not ever."

Marilyn insists that she did nothing to provoke him, that she was a good girl. Even so, the abuse got more and more frightening, until one day he pulled a shotgun on her.

"It was the only time I can ever remember my mother sticking up for me. My father got a gun and aimed it at me. I hadn't done anything wrong, hadn't gone with no boys. He just came home drunk and said he was going to kill me. But my mother pushed him and yelled for me to run out the door, and I did. He took a couple of shots at me, but he didn't hit me."

Her father went to jail that time, she says, but only for a month. It was on the day he returned home that she ran.

"I didn't know what I was going to do, but I got out of there," she says. "I didn't pack anything, didn't take anything with me. I knew if I stayed there, he'd kill me. I knew I had to leave, so I ran. I didn't have a plan or anything. But I don't remember being afraid of being on my own—after all, I'd been getting beat up every day. Running away was no scarier than that."

To the Home School

When she ran from the reservation, Marilyn headed south, to the Twin Cities of Minneapolis and Saint Paul. She had an aunt there who was happy to take her in, she says. Although her aunt had no problems with the arrangement, Marilyn's parents did.

"They sent the police after me, told the authorities I was a runaway," she says. "The police were real nice, but they made me go

Marilyn's early years were filled with unspeakable violence. She recalls, "My father got a gun and aimed it at me. . . . He just came home drunk and said he was going to kill me."

home. Then I'd run away again, come back to Saint Paul. It went on like that for a while.

"It's funny," she says with a bitter laugh. "After a few times of me running away, then being brought back to the reservation, my family got sick of me, too. My father, my brothers, they beat me. It wasn't like they wanted me or anything. They'd say, 'Why don't you go back where you came from?' So I did. I'd hitch rides down to Saint Paul again, and I'd get picked up again. It was dumb, real dumb, the way that kept up.

"Finally, they put me in a government-run school, called a home school. That was north of Saint Paul, in a town called Sauk Centre. The school's still there. It's for girls who are having problems, or who don't have any other place."

Marilyn says that she liked the school at first, because she did not have to worry about running away or being beaten. But as safe as she felt, she found life away from the reservation intimidating.

"I wasn't a good student," she admits with a smile. "I never liked much of anything in school. But in the reservation schools, all the kids were the same—all Ojibwa together. But outside there were minorities and whites, all mixed together. Indian people got called lots of names—drunk Indians, squaw—stuff like that. It hurt when people would say, go back to the reservation where you belong. Especially when my family on the reservation was telling me the same thing: get out of here, go back to the city where you belong. I don't think I knew where I belonged."

"I BECAME A MEAN KID"

Marilyn remembers that many of the girls at the home school had goals: some to get married and have children, others to get a good education so that they could land a well-paid job. She, however, was less hopeful.

"I only wanted to stay there," she says. "Stay there and not get sent back to my father. I don't think I had good goals. I look back on that time and think it was wasted. I mean, the school was okay. There were people who were willing to help. But I kind of wasted my time."

One of Marilyn's problems at the home school was that she had a hard time keeping friends. A sharp tongue and a short temper seemed to drive them away, she says.

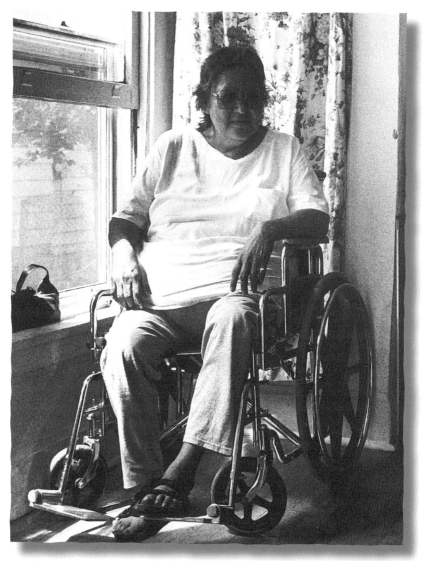

Marilyn's poor health is aggravated by her AIDS condition—sometimes she feels strong, at other times, extremely weak. The condition keeps her from gainful employment.

"I think I turned into a kind of mean kid," she says. "I guess I didn't care too much about too many people, only about myself. I had some friends, but if somebody made me mad, I'd act just like my father did. I didn't hit so much, but I really used my mouth, called people bad names.

"That was hard," says Marilyn, thinking about it. "Some of the girls at the school would tell me how ugly I was when I was mean. But I didn't know how else to be. It's kind of hard to explain now, but it was like there was somebody else inside me, making me do those things. That's how it felt. I finally talked to some of the girls there that I had been bad-mouthing. They sat me down and told me I shouldn't be talking that way, being so mean to people. I learned the hard way, but I learned. At least I had friends that told me before I got myself in a lot of trouble."

Eventually, Marilyn says, she ran from the home school, too.

"I just didn't want to be there," she says. "That's the story of my life, like I said before—running, running, running. Any old problem, and I run. But when I ran back in those days, things always seemed to get worse."

CHILDREN, AND MORE VIOLENCE

While living on her own in Minneapolis, Marilyn was set up on a blind date. The young man's name was Emerson; he was an Indian from Oklahoma.

"That was real important, that he was from another area," she explains. "That means he wasn't related to me. Here in Indian country, Ojibwas are related to everybody else. But he wasn't Ojibwa, he was Chickasaw."

The two got along well, Marilyn says, and they lived together. She had three children with Emerson: a son, Jamie, and two daughters, Lisa and Jennifer. However, as good a man as he first seemed, Emerson started abusing Marilyn, just as her father had.

"We stayed together ten years," she says, "but I spent about six of them trying to get away. Some of the time we lived together; other times he'd move out and stay with friends. But all that time he was mean.

"I don't know what his problem was. He accused me of cheating on him with someone else, but that was crazy, and deep down he must have known it. I was always at home, with my kids. They were everything to me, everything.

"Anyway, he'd come over, start accusing me of things. If the kids and I were gone, he'd break all the windows in the house, steal my groceries, bust up furniture, throw things out the windows. He ripped the phone right out, too. Right out of the wall. He'd do that stuff even if the kids and I were there. They were little, really small then. They saw it all, they stood right there holding on to me, watching him bust up the whole house, break all the windows out. The kids just looked and stood there screaming, just crying and screaming, looking at him do that."

RUNNING AGAIN

Marilyn says that she tried to stop the abuse but that nothing seemed to work.

"Back then, there were no places for women and children to go when they were being abused, not like today. So we did counseling, tried talking things out. But nothing worked, it just kept on. He accused me of terrible things and hit me. I had black eyes, split lips, it seemed like all the time. I used to wake up out of a deep sleep and he'd be there, beating up on me. His fists were huge and really strong. And he'd kick."

Marilyn begins to cry.

"All I ever wanted was my kids. And it was hard when my daughter Lisa cried for her dad. He wasn't a good father, not at all. If he had been, I would never have left him. But I finally got brave and did it. I don't know, I think I'd just had one busted lip too many."

Marilyn says that this time she had a plan. She told her sister that she needed to get a different place to live. Her sister was able to find an apartment in a low-income housing project on the other side of town. If the plan worked, Marilyn thought, she and the children could leave Emerson and he'd be unable to find out where they had gone.

"I did it real good," Marilyn says. "I paid the rent on my place, just like always. That was a time when Emerson was living with us. I arranged to have a moving van come while he was at work at the auto body shop. I got up, made everybody breakfast, just like a regular day. Then, when Emerson left, we packed up everything and took off."

"PEOPLE DON'T CHANGE MUCH"

Marilyn says that it was a good plan and that it would have worked. It *would* have worked had Emerson not been told where Marilyn and their children moved. It still makes her angry, she says, that a mutual acquaintance would have given her secret away.

"Oh, people talk," she says with annoyance. "They tell things. You can't always trust people. That's one thing you always have to remember in life."

Emerson began coming around to her new apartment, and the abuse continued.

"I used to lock him out," she says. "I'd lock the door, and wouldn't care how loud he was in the hall. But if I couldn't get to the door fast enough, and my kids let him in, he'd push right inside and start threatening me. Sometimes he'd break things, like before, sometimes just hit me. Sometimes he brought other guys over there to get rough with me, too."

How it all ended is a puzzle Marilyn has yet to understand.

"I told him one day, flat out, that I couldn't take no more. I can't do it, I said, I don't want to be hit or punched or pounded on. It was over, I said. I didn't want him around ever again."

She shakes her head as though baffled by the success of her speech.

The father of Marilyn's children continued the cycle of abuse she became familiar with as a child: "Sometimes he'd break things . . . sometimes just hit me. Sometimes he brought other guys over there to get rough with me, too."

"He tried threatening me a little, telling me that he better not find out there was somebody else. He said he didn't want to be the last one to know, if there was.

"That was all," she says. "He stopped coming around. I don't know, even now, what made him stop. For some reason, just telling him that enough was enough, that got through to him, where he never seemed to believe me before. Or maybe I had never told him those words before, I don't know."

Marilyn says that she never sees Emerson anymore, even though they live in the same city.

"I know he could still be mine if I wanted him," she says. "Which I don't. For some reason, he believes that he loves me. But I hear he is beating up on the woman he's with now. People don't change much. The part that doesn't seem fair is that he has a nice place to live. He beats people up and he's got a home. I'm the one who's homeless. It doesn't seem right."

"THE HITTING STARTED . . . IT DIDN'T STOP"

Marilyn's decision to rid her life of Emerson was a positive one, she says, but what happened afterwards turned out to be a nightmare for her family, one that haunts her family even today.

"I was raising my kids on my own," she says, "working a little, getting some welfare money for the kids. We weren't doing great, but we were getting by. I met another man, and my relationship with him turned out to be a tragedy.

"His name was Art," she says quietly, looking down at her lap. "He turned out to be mean to me, but meaner to my kids. I saw him take after my son Jamie when Jamie was in fourth grade. He meant to hurt Jamie. My daughter, too. He went after both of them with fists.

"I didn't know he was that way at first. He seemed okay, not like Emerson. But the hitting started, and once it started, it didn't stop. I remember blocking punches—hard ones—meant for my kids. I took them myself."

Marilyn says she has heard all the stories about children who've been abused, how they turn out to be abusive parents themselves. She disagrees with the statistics, she says, for in her case it just wasn't true.

"There was no way that I was going to let my kids get hit," she whispers, still looking down. "I was glad to block the punches. I wasn't going to let that happen to Jamie, Jennifer, and Lisa, what my father had done to me. I didn't want them to feel that way.

"I left, but it wasn't soon enough. I thought that by blocking the punches I was protecting my kids, but the punches were only part of the problem. There was abuse going on that I didn't know about, and that was the tragedy."

Marilyn relates, with great difficulty, the horror she felt when she found out that for years Art had been having sex with her daughter Lisa.

"I was with him for five years," she says. "When he started having sex with her, Lisa didn't tell us. She was only five when it started, and she was scared. He had told her that if she told anyone, he'd kill her mother and the rest of her family. I guess things had been going on like that for years before I found out. I walked in a room, and there he was, taking Lisa's pants off. "

Marilyn sobs, unable to catch her breath.

"She was just a little girl, just a little ten-year-old girl."

"EVERYTHING BAD WAS IN OUR FAMILY"

Marilyn got her children to a crisis center and told them not to come home until she contacted them.

"I got to work and I was too upset. I told my foreman that I was having a personal problem and I needed to see someone. He sent me to a counselor, who helped me decide to press charges against Art for what he'd done to Lisa.

"He was convicted," she says, "and got four and a half years for what he did. It was not enough time for all that he did to mess up my daughter's life. Not nearly enough time. I mean, he'd been raping her, over and over for five years. It wasn't fair, the sentence he got."

Lisa underwent years of counseling, says Marilyn, and it helped a little. However, the pain and anguish of it all proved too much for Marilyn and her family.

"We just fell apart," she says, closing her eyes. "I knew Lisa was hurting. The sexual abuse was haunting her every place she went. I knew she was in pain, but I didn't know what to do with her. I felt anger and hurt and shame. I felt that I should have known. I would have protected her if I'd known.

"So everybody in our family got into their own lives, trying to keep the hurt away. Everybody did what they wanted, there was no talking, no sharing anymore. Drinking, drugs, staying out late, whatever. I mean, we weren't mean to each other, but there was no family either. No one listened to anyone else. Yeah, guilt, embarrassment, shame—everything bad was in our family."

RUNNING AGAIN

So, Marilyn says, they ran away. They all went to Chicago—a change of scene, a place none of them had been before. She had a sister who lived there, so they knew they'd have a place to sleep when they first arrived.

"We stayed with her for a little while," says Marilyn. "After a while I found my own place. But nothing really improved. A new city, new buildings, new streets, but the same old hurt.

"The family was pretty well shot by that time," she shrugs. "We still were drinking, carrying on. I'd always been a drinker, and I

Marilyn dates her second relationship as the final breakdown of her tenuous family life. After he sexually abused one of her daughters, her family "just fell apart . . . I knew Lisa was hurting. The sexual abuse was haunting her every place she went."

got into it heavier than ever then. Drugs, too. I'd never really used drugs before that time. And I got into it big time, not just marijuana, but crack, cocaine, lots of stuff. I was injecting drugs, too—heroin especially."

Where did she get the money for all these drugs? Marilyn smiles sadly.

"It's easy to get high for free, if you really want to," she says. "You'd be surprised how many people will share. No one likes to get high alone, especially on heroin."

It didn't take long for Jamie and Jennifer to realize they didn't want to be in Chicago. Marilyn says they were wise, that they all should have left.

"Jamie was the first to leave," she says. "He ran away back to Minneapolis to be with his friends. He left on Christmas Eve. Jennifer was next. She told me one day that she was going home for a visit then packed up all her stuff and left. She never came back. So she got out. It was just Lisa and I then. We were the foolish ones."

Lisa and her mother continued their drug use, with Lisa more heavily into heroin than her mother.

"She was using everything," Marilyn remembers grimly. "She used it all. Toward the end she was even sniffing paint thinner—anything to get high."

SPLITTING UP THE FAMILY

While she and her mother were in Chicago, Lisa had two babies—Desirae and Robert. Marilyn says that Lisa was too involved with drugs to be a good mother in Chicago, so she herself had to be the primary caregiver.

"She wanted to be a good mother, I think," says Marilyn, "but the drugs were too powerful. She was never home. Off she'd go, and we'd never hear from her. And the father of the kids wasn't any kind of real father. I was the only one looking out for those kids.

"I still did drugs a little, but I had to watch it, like I said, because I was all Desirae and Robert had. And after a while, it just seemed like life wasn't ever going to get no better unless I left. That city wasn't good for me, wasn't good for any of us."

Marilyn tried to persuade Lisa to let her take Desirae and Robert back to Minneapolis with her, but Lisa refused. Finally, Lisa relented and allowed Desirae to leave. Robert would stay with her in Chicago. But as Marilyn says, it was an arrangement that was bound to fail.

"I left with Desirae. It was 1988. She and her brother were still real little, preschoolers I think. I was so worried about Lisa and Robert; I couldn't imagine how they were going to make it. I kept wondering, is Lisa paying any attention to that boy? Is anybody home to take care of him, to cook him breakfast? I worried so much that Desirae and I kept making bus trips down to Chicago, checking up on them."

A NEW BEGINNING

On one of her trips back to Chicago, Marilyn saw that Lisa was not going to survive the life that she'd chosen.

"It was bad for her, bad for the boy," she says, shaking her head. "I said, 'Come on, Lisa, let's start over. Let's go back to Minneapolis, all of us, and make a new beginning. We'll get off the booze, get off the drugs.'"

Marilyn says that she was not surprised when Lisa agreed.

"She knew she was an addict, " says Marilyn. "She couldn't keep it up that way. And she knew this was no life for a little boy, off by himself all the time while she was getting high. Deep down, Lisa had sense. It was just those drugs; they got her every time."

True to her word, Marilyn stopped using drugs when she came back to Minneapolis, and Lisa stopped, too. They stayed for a while with one of Marilyn's brothers in the city; later they found a place of their own.

"It was a good idea, having a new beginning," says Marilyn. "But the sad thing was, we really couldn't have a beginning. Some things from the past, from the bad time, interfered. We found out that we couldn't start over, not at all."

"IF I GOT IT, YOU GOT IT"

One of the things Marilyn wanted to do to start off her new beginning was to get tested at a clinic to make sure she hadn't contracted HIV or any other diseases while she was on drugs.

"I knew it was a possibility," she says, "but I wanted to make sure I was okay. I wanted to really start off clean, start the right way. It was not the doctor's idea, or anything, just mine.

"Anyway, Lisa and the kids were in the room with me when I got the call from the clinic. The nurse on the line asked if I was sitting down, and I told her no. She said, 'Sit down; we've got some bad news, Marilyn.' Then she told me the AIDS test had come back positive. I remember just sitting there, feeling like the world was crashing down on me.

"I told Lisa that she'd better go in, too. If I got it, you got it, I told her. We'd been sharing needles, her and I. We'd lived the same kind of life in Chicago. Lisa didn't want to find out; it took her a while before she got brave enough to go in. She didn't want to face it. But the news was as bad for her as it was for me."

Lisa took the news harder than Marilyn had. She was devastated, and it was all Marilyn could do to keep her daughter from withdrawing completely.

"She was completely thrown. Back then an AIDS diagnosis meant you were going to die fast. There weren't as many medicines as there are now to prolong things. She got knocked down by the disease, knocked down by the news. Her attitude was negative, so I think that's why she'd been much sicker with AIDS than I've been."

Marilyn sits with grandson Robert, who has been violent toward his mother, Lisa, far right. Lisa also suffers from the fatigue of AIDS.

"A Little Voice Wouldn't Let Me Go Home"

Although the living arrangements seemed fine at first, it soon became apparent that Marilyn and Lisa were not going to be able to stay together under one roof. That became obvious in April, when Marilyn left, becoming a homeless person.

"It didn't work with all of us," Marilyn says, fiddling with a soggy piece of Kleenex in her lap. "Lisa and I don't agree on how those kids should be raised. We ended up getting in a fight—I mean, a big old fight, not just a disagreement.

"The problem is that there are too many bosses. No one agrees, and the kids play us against each other. Lisa, I think, tries hard to be a good mother. She's not on any drugs or anything. But sometimes she ignores them when they act bad, and they do plenty of that. Sometimes it's easier for her—with her being so sick and all—to let it happen, to just give in and do the easy thing. But it isn't right."

Marilyn says that she didn't tell anyone about her plan to leave.

"Earlier in the day I was talking to Lisa," she remembers. "I was telling her that I was very dissatisfied with the way our lives

Although Marilyn and Lisa have tried to live together, they eventually agreed that Marilyn should leave. "Lisa and I don't agree on how those kids should be raised."

Marilyn receives free bus tokens at the shelter. Marilyn takes the bus to "stop at Lisa's place, and make phone calls. . . . I don't live there, but I go there almost every day."

were going. Too many hurtful things were going on, and no one was standing up against it. She didn't need me there, didn't want me there any more than I wanted to be there. I needed my own place, but I didn't have one; that was the bad part. And then I had a doctor's appointment, and a little voice or something wouldn't let me go home. It's hard to explain. It was just a little voice inside me that said, 'Don't go back.'"

HOMELESS

Marilyn joined her other daughter, Jennifer, who was also home-less at the time. Jennifer was at a shelter, and she sneaked her mother in there for a few nights.

"Then she introduced me to a woman at the shelter who kind of ran things, and this lady was able to put me up. It wasn't very nice there. The room was terribly moldy; I was sneezing and coughing all night. I borrowed an electric frying pan and cooked a little bit there. But it was temporary, you know what I mean? I guess everything is temporary when you got no place that's yours. I'm at another shelter now, a nicer one. But it's still temporary. I've got to be out next week. Then, who knows?"

Marilyn tries to keep a routine to her days, unlike many of the people she sees at the shelter.

"I get up with the birds," she smiles. "I'm up by 5:00 or 5:30. I wait around until the girl that works at the shelter gets here. Her name is Shelley, and she lets us have free bus tokens. That way I can go off on my rounds.

"I wander around, see some people I've met, go outside and smoke, since you can't smoke inside this shelter. I talk to a few of the people here at the shelter, but I mostly stay to myself. I take the bus, stop at Lisa's place, and make phone calls. Sure, I still can

Marilyn has tried to step in to do some of the mothering of Robert, who is violent and unpredictable. "I just keep after him, keep talking until he hears me . . . [until] he's relaxed, lying on the couch, calling me Grandma again."

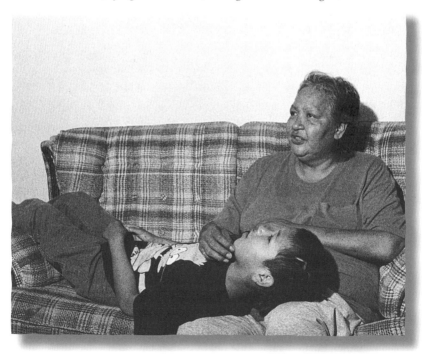

go to Lisa's. I don't live there, but I go there almost every day. I help out. They're my family; they're all I've got. Just because it isn't my home don't mean they don't like to see me for a little while each day.

"Anyway, I see Lisa and the kids. I try to look around for a place that I can live in. It's hard now, because I don't feel well lots of the time. I don't have a lot of energy, especially when the weather is hot, like now. I don't have a lot of money, either, and that's hard when you need to find an apartment. But you know, it's so hard not to have a home."

Where does she eat? Marilyn shrugs.

"I eat a little here and there. Sometimes I go to the soup line, but usually not. I don't feel right asking. I buy a little sometimes, sometimes get a meal or a sandwich at Lisa's or a friend's. Not real regular, but enough to get by, you know?"

Marilyn's eyes fill up with tears.

"I'm not a street person. There aren't many of those around here. Mostly everyone can get into some kind of shelter, at least for a few days. Then you move on. But it's hard for me to ask for things. I feel like a beggar, and that's no way to be."

Keeping Control

Interestingly, Marilyn still takes an active role with Robert and Desirae, even though she no longer lives there. She talks with pride about Desirae's summer job, a job she herself lined up.

"It's a youth program thing, helping at the zoo," says Marilyn, smiling. "I helped Desirae fill out the application and everything. I told her that even though she's got this job, she has to be good about doing her chores. Her mother can't do too much, so Desirae's got to help out. I told her that if she ignored those chores, she'd have to quit that job and work here in the house for no pay."

Marilyn is glad that her granddaughter is gone much of the day, for the job keeps her busy and out of trouble. If only she could get eleven-year-old Robert into something like that, she says ruefully.

"He's the one I really worry over," Marilyn says. "He's mouthy; he gives Lisa lots of trouble. A whole lot of wild, that's Robert. He's a loner, so we can't blame the kids he hangs around with. He's always had trouble making friends. He acts mouthy and mean, and then people don't want to get to know him. I guess that sounds like somebody else I know, huh?"

Marilyn tries to make up for Lisa's lack of energy, taking the brunt of Robert's anger, just as she used to block the punches meant for Lisa and her other children when they were little.

"I don't really have any control, but I've got lots of energy where that boy is concerned," she says. "I just keep after him, keep talking until he hears me. He tells me to shut up. I say, 'Oh, thank you anyway, Robert, but you're going to have to listen.' He calls me bitch, and I say, 'Oh, thank you, Robert, I love those words you call me.'

"So by the time we get done with all of that, he's relaxed, lying on the couch, calling me Grandma again. [Dealing with Robert is] something Lisa can't do, like I told you before. She's just not feeling well enough to do that."

"I Think I Made Her Mad, but It's Not the First Time"

Marilyn feels a special bond with Lisa, too, even though the two fight over even the smallest thing. And even though, admits Marilyn, that it is her failing relationship with Lisa that has resulted in her being homeless.

"I tell her what's on my mind," Marilyn says firmly. "She needs to hear things from me. I love her, but I hate to see her, the way she's dealing with AIDS. She looks awful—gray face, sunken-in eyes. We had a talk about it the other night.

"Lisa doesn't think she can live, and she doesn't give herself a chance to. She has decided that she will die soon. I told her that all these things that she thinks about, they will happen that way. The power of the mind is strong. I told her, 'If I were you, I'd get on the ball and change my attitude right now.'

"She doesn't take her medicine, and that's wrong. She needs it, because she's got some microbacteria in her lungs, something that's really making her sick. She says she doesn't like the way the medicine makes her feel. 'Well, too bad,' I told her. 'You're not God that you can be messing around with your life that way. You say you love life, you say you love your kids; then your chance to show it is now. Right now. Think positive.'"

Marilyn knows that Lisa gets angry when her mother lectures her, but she doesn't care.

"I think I made her mad, but it's not the first time," she says. "Jennifer and Jamie were there when we were talking, and they agreed with me. They told Lisa she needs to think positively. That's the only way to feel better. Besides, I'm her mother, and she's my daughter. There's a bond there that no one can take away, not even by a quarrel."

"I'D BE DREAMING"

People who don't know homeless people might think they are lazy, mentally ill, or chemically dependent, says Marilyn. People might think that their only goals are to get high or to sit around all day waiting for a handout.

Marilyn is proud of her granddaughter Desirae, who seems to already have a firm desire to escape poverty. Marilyn says: "If I were Desirae's age right now, I'd be dreaming of being a doctor."

"But that's not me," she insists. "I have goals. They may not sound like a whole lot to anybody with a nice house, a good education, a car. But they are important to me. I want my family to get along. I want my grandkids acting good, acting nice. I want them all to be together, to be loyal to one another."

Marilyn's voice dwindles to a whisper.

"But it's so hard to see them now, see the way they act. I don't like to see those kids growing up in this kind of a world, all the things that go on—the AIDS, the poverty."

Marilyn says she is hopeful in some ways, because she knows there are things kids have now that were not available to her when she was a troubled teenager.

"There are all kinds of advantages—even to poor kids, abused kids," she says. "There are crisis centers, counselors that can help. Even in the schools, there are people who will listen to kids if they have something to say. That's real good. I wish I'd had something like that."

What if she were able to start over—what would she want for her life?

"If I were Desirae's age right now," she smiles, "I'd be dreaming of being a doctor. Any kind of doctor, just so I was helping people. I'd like to live out in the country somewhere, where there was lots of space, just helping people feel better.

"I used to think about that when I was a girl, too," she remembers. "When I was at the home school, I'd think about being a doctor. But they said once you got that runaway label on your record, you can't be doing things like being a doctor. I know now that isn't so, but I believed them."

Sometimes Marilyn dreams about returning to White Earth, to the reservation. It is a place Robert might enjoy, she says.

"Maybe that would be a home for me, I don't know," she thinks aloud. "It would be good for Robert—a lot of open space, open country. He could swim, climb trees, be as wild as he feels like.

"The thing is, though, the reservation is not a place to stay. Especially when you got your whole life ahead. There are no dreams there, no future. The dreams are all outside. It was my own fault that I never did anything with those dreams. I just didn't work hard enough, I guess."

Ben and Ann

"I AM NOT IN THE HABIT OF ASKING FOR FOOD, BEGGING FOR A ROOF OVER MY HEAD—NOT FROM A STRANGER."

"Talk about being in the wrong place at the wrong time," Ann says with barely suppressed rage. "The story of our family gives new meaning to the idea of bad luck."

Ann is in her mid-thirties, an attractive woman with a wide smile and an engaging manner. But she is doing little smiling these days, she admits.

"Six weeks ago Ben and I were living in a big old house in the city," she says. "At night we tucked our kids into bed, safe and sound. We had backyard barbecues and had friends come over for the evening. If you had asked me six weeks ago, I'd have said life was fine. I mean, life was fine."

But several weeks ago, everything changed. One evening in late spring, an evening that still gives the family nightmares, the police raided their home, trying to capture a man believed to be a murderer. In the raid, their home was destroyed.

"Our furniture, the kids' toys, our clothes—everything was ruined," she says bitterly. "What wasn't destroyed by the bullets was splattered with that tear gas, and you can't get the smell out, no matter what. And then, what wasn't ruined that way was looted out of the house afterwards, after the police got through with the place."

And now, says Ann's husband, Ben, they are homeless.

"We're down in the shelter now," he says, his voice cracking with emotion. "We are victims of circumstance. We are in no way responsible for what happened to us. Yet here we are with the drug addicts, the ignorant people, the drunks, the prostitutes. I don't have any money. We have no car. Every bit of savings we had has been used up.

"I feel so bad for my family, so ashamed of where we live. I mean, do we want our kids to look back on their childhood and remember this? Living in shelters? Standing in line for a meal that we can't pay for?

"This isn't right. Ann knows it; I know it. We have higher dreams for our family. But you know, right now, there's not a damned thing I can do about it."

Ben and Ann are eager to get out of the homeless shelter they find themselves in. "We have higher dreams for our family."

Ben grew up in a high-crime neighborhood, but managed to want something better for himself. "My mother was a big force in my life. . . . She sent me to good schools, took an interest in my learning."

"MOST OF MY RELATIVES ARE CRIMINALS"

Ben is a handsome black man with the posture and bearing of a soldier. He is tall and muscular, and looks far younger than his fifty years.

"I did serve in the Marine Corps, for six and a half years," he says proudly, clearly relieved to be talking of something other than his family's homelessness. "I did three and a half years in Vietnam, and I came away from that with shrapnel in my back and legs. I don't walk so well. I get sore really fast. It's hard to reach or to pick up anything heavy."

Ben says that his time in the marines taught him discipline and honor, two ingredients that were missing from most of the people in his family.

"I'm from Detroit originally," he explains. "There, in Detroit, my last name is synonymous with crime. Lots of people in my

35

family—most of my relatives, in fact—are in prison or dead because of being connected with crime. I knew when I was pretty young that I didn't want to be like them.

"My mother was a big force in my life, though. She sent me to good schools, took an interest in my learning. I did ROTC in school, all that stuff. I never had a police record, never had a problem with the law.

"On the other hand," he says with a sad smile, "I have a brother in prison for murder, a sister into drugs. But I've got another sister, Alice, who is an excellent person. She owns her own beauty salon. Alice has lots of pride in herself. I named our daughter after her. I don't know . . . Alice and I had the same mother as the others, but I think we must have learned the right things at the right time. I guess we were the only ones."

A Different Background

Ann's background is far different from her husband's. Like him, she was born and raised in Detroit. However, her family is comprised of many professional people—and no criminals.

"We have lots of lawyers, teachers, and preachers in our family," she says, smiling. "Lots of well-educated people. And boy, when they heard I was marrying Ben, there were some fireworks! His last name, like he told you, is a crime name in Detroit, so my family was like, 'You're marrying that boy, and look at what his family is! How can you think of doing that?'"

Ben grins and takes her hand.

"After they got to know me, they knew I wasn't like the rest of my family," he says. "They are a little hesitant about me, even now, but I've never given them any reason to doubt me, to doubt that I'm a good man."

On the Right Side of the Law

One way that Ben has demonstrated his upstanding nature is by working closely with the police, both in Detroit and in Minneapolis.

"If I could choose a career, I'd be a police officer," Ben says wistfully. "I couldn't pass the physical, though, because of being wounded in Vietnam. But I *can* do the next best thing: join the police reserves. That's what I did—eleven years with the reserves in Detroit.

"I feel that what they do is so important. The crime where we lived in Detroit was unbelievable. Crack houses every place—it's like an epidemic. I felt that to be a responsible citizen it was important to help them any way I could. I mean, it was important just because I lived in the neighborhood and I had a wife and children, you know?"

Part of the work Ben did in the reserves was to let the police know about crack houses operating in the neighborhood and even to work undercover in some situations.

"I helped the police by pretending to make drug buys," says Ben. "I was even awarded the Citizens' Award of Valor for closing down so many of those crack houses."

Ben holds a plaque he received for working in the police reserves. "If I could choose a career, I'd be a police officer."

"You know," says Ann quietly, "it was drugs that made us leave Detroit, drugs and the violence that go with [them]. We left Detroit three days after a third grader in my son Benjamin's class got shotgunned to death. It was over narcotics . . . can you even believe what I'm saying? A third grader, nine years old, shot down and killed right in class. We lived near the school; I could hear the shots from my kitchen."

"We did get out of there fast," says Ben. "I couldn't even imagine staying. Detroit has the reputation of being the murder capital of the world. I don't know if that's true, but when they start knocking off third graders, you know, what's next?"

LEAVING HOME

Ben and Ann say that they had nothing lined up in Minneapolis before they arrived. They knew it had a good reputation—good schools, strong communities. Perhaps, they admit now, they were too anxious to believe only the good things.

Ben and Ann share a strong commitment to their children and family. "We are a Muslim family," Ben says. "Discipline is no stranger to this family."

"We came here like we were making a pilgrimage to Mecca, you know?" says Ann, smiling ruefully. "We'd heard things like, you can leave your doors unlocked, and not worry about anything. We even had somebody tell us that there weren't any rats or roaches here, that it was too cold in the winter! No gangs or violence, we heard. A small amount of drugs, things like that."

"Yeah, right," says Ben sarcastically. "We heard what we wanted to hear. Hey, some of those same faces I helped put behind bars back in Detroit are here, selling drugs in this city, down on Lake and Chicago Avenue. I know it's better here, nothing like Detroit, but there are lots of problems. Anytime you got crack, you got a world of problems.

"It's not the whole black community," he says seriously, "but it's a good number, you know? It's enough to make some people look at the black people in this city and say we're all a bunch of dope fiends. It's bad. Even where we lived, in our house that got shot up, there was a crack house next door, a crack house across the street. The neighborhood we were living in was called the Phillips neighborhood, the largest in the city, and it has 197 crack houses. That's as of last October. I guess it's a fact of life. A sad fact of life."

MAKING A HOME

The family stayed with relatives for a short while then decided to get a place of their own. It was a welcome change, Ann remembers.

"No matter how nice your relatives are, it's not fun to be staying too long," she says. "And these were relatives of Ben's, not too happy that he was a police reservist, you know? It was kind of the opposite of how things should have been. I mean, they treated him as if he were a criminal. He was on the wrong side of the law, maybe—the wrong side from where they stood."

Ben and Ann soon found a beautiful old house to rent in the Phillips neighborhood. The house was full of rich woodwork, big windows to let the light in, and a lovely wraparound porch.

"It was a dream house," says Ann. "It had everything we'd wanted. Lots of space for the kids to play, lots of rooms for Ben's books and computers, lots of windows for our plants to grow."

"I was doing some undercover work for the police. Nothing steady, but something to do," says Ben. "But then I was approached by community leaders. They were interested in me as a neighborhood liaison person between the community and the police. There were some troubles in Phillips, and maybe I could help.

"I got the job, and I loved it," he says. "I was getting to be close with some of the gang leaders, talking to them about things, just about their lives, what they were into. Some of them were interested that I was a Muslim, and they wanted to know more about that. A few of them even embraced Islam after talking to me about the ideas of the religion.

"And sometimes our talks were just neighborhood stuff, about easing up, staying out of some of the parks, you know. It's a slow process, but an important one. It's important for these guys to understand that people are willing to talk to them. It's easy to get angry, but that won't solve the problems in the communities. We have to just stay focused and work on one problem at a time, so that was my job."

Then, when Ann landed a teaching assistant's job at Head Start, the family really felt that things were looking up.

"I was working. Ben was working," she says. "We just felt like we were in a good place, you know?"

She closes her eyes, as though it was painful to remember all of this.

"But we didn't know what was going to happen, or we would have never felt so secure. We would have been ready for the bad that was getting ready to happen."

"HE'D MURDERED SOME PEOPLE, AND NOW HE'S IN MY ATTIC"

The trouble began when a young man Ben and Ann knew arrived at their home late one night and asked if he could spend the night.

"His name was Jojo," says Ben. "We didn't know him well, but he was one of those young guys I'd been talking to in the neighborhood. He had a friend with him, a guy we hadn't seen before. Jojo introduced him as Dray. But we told them they could stay, [that] we were glad to see them. Besides, we had a big house, lots of room."

Ben says that no alarms went off for him. Nothing seemed out of the ordinary—even when Dray gave Ben a gun.

"That was totally appropriate," Ben explains. "Like I said, we're a Muslim home. Jojo had embraced Islam, so he knew the rules.

When you enter a Muslim home, you surrender your weapon to your host. That's the way it is."

Did he not think it suspicious that Dray had a weapon at all? Ben laughs, shaking his head.

"Not in the least," he says. "Look, there is so much crime in the black community, so many black males killing each other. If I were a young kid now, living in that place with all that's going on, I'd probably be carrying a pistol, too, out of fear of losing my life. Your life is in danger constantly. That's a fact. Some other young guy, some gang member, some drugged-out guy wanting your wallet. Not unusual.

"So I wasn't even worried," he continues. "Just put the pistol under my mattress and went back to sleep. Next day, nothing much going on. That night we barbecued on the grill, the family and our two guests."

Trouble began, says Ann, when the police showed up.

Ben and Ann's children continue to be traumatized by the destruction of their home, although they are continually comforted and cared for by their parents.

"We were eating," she says, "and all of a sudden the boy Dray noticed them outside. He ran right upstairs, didn't say anything to anyone. Ran right up to the attic on the third floor."

"We went outside," says Ben, "and were talking to the police. As it turns out, Dray is wanted by the police, because they say he killed some people on a farm outside of the city. He'd murdered some people, and now he's in my attic. I knew where the boy had run to, and I told the police—pointed it out to them, just where the window of the attic was."

A ONE-WAY SHOOTOUT

"The whole thing was so stupid," says Ben. "The police asked some of the neighbors to take us in while the whole incident was going down. I kept telling the police, 'Just set off a couple of canisters in the attic, that should do the trick.'

"I told the police that the boy wasn't armed. I knew that, because he'd given me a gun to hold, and I was sure he hadn't had another. It turned out I was right: they caught him unarmed. But not before they'd destroyed the house with that stupid gas."

"It was a crime," says Ann, clearly upset by the memory. "The police just started shooting. They were the only ones shooting, too. Every time we heard a shot, we'd just jump. The kids were terrified."

"Me? I kept hearing those shots of tear gas, and the tears were just streaming down my face," admits Ben. "Like I said, they needed two. They shot in between 150 and 200. What was that for? You tell me, what was that for?"

The destruction seemed almost purposeful to Ann, who heard members of the police SWAT team making racist comments as they surrounded the house.

"This is what makes me so angry," says Ann, her voice angry. "You say, am I mad? Yeah, I'm mad. I'm so mad I don't trust myself, if some police officer walked in this room. I'd tell him, yes I would.

"Those SWAT guys, white men, were saying, 'Hey, let's just get the nigger's house.' Oh, I wish I'd had a badge number. You bet I'd report it. I'm a bitter woman. How this city, this police department, can pretend to honor Ben, to thank him for that dangerous work—going undercover in drug buys, helping negotiate with gangs. How they can do that and say they didn't know it was his house they were shooting up. Oh, *please*. *Please*, don't give me any of that, 'cause I ain't buying it."

The discussion has been too much. Ben retreats to his room, unwilling and unable to talk more. Another day, he says. Just not now. Ann, tears rolling down her cheeks, follows her husband inside the shelter.

ANOTHER DAY

Today the children have come downstairs. They are eager for a ride in a car. It's been a while since they've been anywhere except close by the shelter.

Benjamin is big for eight years old. He has his father's bright smile and is quick to shake hands with a visitor. His little sisters, Alice, age five, and Fatima, age four, are dressed in matching shorts and shirts, their thick hair braided and ribboned.

"We'll take you to the house so you can see it yourself," announces their father cheerfully, as though it was no longer a painful subject. "You can see what kind of damage we had."

Benjamin looks troubled. He whispers to his father that he doesn't really want to go back there. He is afraid, he says. Couldn't he stay here with Mama?

"Your mama's coming, too," says Ben. "It'll be okay, Benjamin. We won't go inside."

The house is just minutes from the shelter. The children and Ann crowd in the backseat of the little car; Ben sits up front with the driver. He points out nearby crack houses. Some have already been raided and boarded up; others seem to be doing a lively business. Black youths cruise by slowly in old cars, watching with expressionless faces as Ben and his family gaze at their house.

GOING HOME

It is huge, with bright yellow siding. Except for the many chinks and holes left by the bullets and the tear gas canisters, the siding looks brand new. Windows are boarded up with the same blond plywood that has been nailed over the crack houses in the neighborhood.

"Terrible sight," says Ben as he picks his way carefully through the broken glass near the base of the house. "This is so painful, you just can't believe. I mean, we had things people dream about owning, things we saved for years to buy. Antiques, quilts, books, nice furniture. Things our parents and grandparents had passed on to us, you know? Things maybe other people wouldn't value in the same way we would, but really important things.

"And my plants!" Ben groans. "Man, I can't believe it; I feel almost fatherly about those plants. Everything was just destroyed, ruined by that gas. Everything that was in the house smells like it. You can't even go in there without masks on, and gloves. It gets

The family looks at the home that the SWAT team destroyed. Ann says, "The police just started shooting. They were the only ones shooting, too. Every time we heard a shot, we'd just jump. The kids were terrified."

right in your face, breaks you out, you know? Everything we picked up in there, we put in plastic bags, and put it in storage."

"The clothes we tried to wash," said Ann, "but it's a joke. I mean, you wash, you wash, you wash it again, and it still has that burning smell. And it leaves a pink goopy stuff on everything. The gas is pink, and you just can't get it off.

"One thing that really made me sad was that I'd bought the kids some back-to-school clothes. It was in the spring, but I'd just gotten paid from my teaching job, and I don't work in the summer. So I thought, why not get the stuff ahead of time, now, while I've got the extra money? So I bought wool skirts, some nice sweaters, even coats for the kids."

She rolls her eyes and shakes her head.

"That was so depressing; all that stuff ruined. It was like throwing money away, you know?"

"I Don't Have That Bed Anymore"

Little Fatima is running around the yard, loudly complaining about all the trash there.

"That wasn't here before, was it, Mama?" she asks with annoyance. "We didn't have pop bottles in our grass."

Benjamin is not talking. He has found a large stick and is banging it against the house, against the big cottonwood trees in the backyard.

Fatima lists toys she has lost: her Barbies, her baby dolls, all her doll clothes and the toy dog that sat on her bed. Alice is mad about her books and her dolls. Benjamin mumbles that his Power Rangers are lost, and the major league baseball locker he got when Minnesota Twins star Kirby Puckett came to their neighborhood once for a crime prevention meeting.

Fatima remembers that there used to be a white squirrel that lived in their cottonwood tree. Maybe it's still there, she says, and begins looking around. Benjamin tells her no, that the police probably shot the squirrel. Fatima looks sad and walks over to her mother.

Alice is pointing out where her room was.

"That was my bedroom," she says. "I had my dolls in there, and my Lion King cup. And my mama used to tuck me in at night, back when I was little. She'd say, 'Goodnight, my little princess.'"

She chews on her lip thoughtfully.

"We can't do that anymore though," she says. "I don't have that bed anymore, so my mama can't tuck me in. That other bed's all shot up with bullets and tear gas. My dad even saw it."

"Discipline Is No Stranger to This Family"

The ride back to the shelter is more somber. Seeing their old house was confusing to the children, and their mother understands their feelings. She suggests stopping for a Popsicle at a corner grocery, and the children perk up a little.

Benjamin walks quickly to a shelf of jumbo-sized candy bars, choosing a Butterfinger. Ann tells him no, to find a Popsicle. Reluctantly he moves to the ice cream case and picks out an ice cream bar coated with fudge and nuts. Ann shakes her head and talks quietly to him.

"You know, Benjamin, you don't really want to eat this, do you? This old fudge thing? You know you don't like it when the kids call you fat. This chocolate is going to just make things worse, you know. Come on, Ben, how about a Popsicle like your sisters have?"

Ben looks distressed. He *likes* to eat, he tells his mother. She seems about to relent until he catches sight of his father. Ben gives his son a stern look and shakes his head.

"Yes, Daddy," Ben says glumly, and puts the ice cream bar back.

"Discipline," says Ben, giving Benjamin a quick hug. "We are a Muslim family, like I said. Discipline is no stranger to this family. That's a religion based on lots of self-discipline, respect for your body and your mind. Choosing the right diet, the right behavior patterns—all those things give you control. And control is what gives you the strength to be strong in your values, in the way you conduct yourself."

We're the Last Ones Who Need Reminding

It is their religion, says Ben, that gives them strength, but it is also what makes their stay in the shelter so humiliating.

"We are required to follow so many rules here," he complains. "It's like a jail. Everyone must be in by 9:00 at night, and they have bed checks to make sure nobody is taking a night out. Then they come around the next morning, making sure everybody's up and dressed, and the place is getting cleaned up."

He smiles sadly.

"I understand why they do it," he admits, "considering the kind of people you have here. You need tight rules, lots of discipline, or they'll run this place into the ground. But it isn't necessary for us."

Ann agrees.

"I feel so funny when the staff comes in and makes sure we're all up in the morning. I mean, we're up at 4:30 every morning, because we pray then. We get up early then, to wash before we pray.

Because Ben and Ann have a tight-knit family, they bristle at some of the rules at the shelter. "It's like a jail. Everyone must be in by 9:00 at night, and they have bed checks to make sure nobody is taking a night out."

We believe you have to be clean to pray before God. Sometimes we wake the kids up to pray then, sometimes we just let them sleep. But Ben and I pray every morning early, no matter what.

"So to have someone coming in to check on us to see if we're still lounging around in bed at 10:00 in the morning, it's an insult. Look at our girls. Their hair is braided up nice, their clothes are clean and ironed, their hands are washed. Some people maybe need to be told to make their kids change their underwear or wash their fingernails. We don't."

Ben says that Islam sometimes has an undeserved reputation for being harsh and repressive.

"Some Muslims are cold; some do things we would consider mean," he says. "But that's a cultural thing, not a religious thing. We choose to practice the type of Islam known as the Way of the Prophet. The idea of this type of Islam is to obey the law, to have a strong sense of family and the values that make families strong, and to be nonviolent.

"That's what we want our kids to learn," says Ben. "We want them to grow up knowing they have a proud heritage and a lot to live up to. There are good examples in this world, and I hope my children follow them."

"I Am Not in the Habit of Asking for Food"

As difficult an adjustment as the shelter has been, both Ann and Ben agree that it has been a lifesaver.

"As shelters go, this is the top of the line," Ann says. "We both know that, and we are grateful that they let us in here. One place where we were at first was a nightmare: drugs, prostitutes, all kinds of stuff. The first night we were there, the girls found a crack pipe under the bed."

She shakes her head.

"No, thank you. And then we met the lady that runs this place. I knew about her, knew she was really religious. I had no intention of asking her for anything. I am not in the habit of asking for food, begging for a roof over my head—not from a stranger.

"Listen," she says, wagging her finger, "if I had to go begging, I'd call up my family. They could afford to help us out. But I don't want to give them the satisfaction of saying 'We told you that Ben was trouble.' No, I won't do that. The price of asking my family is too great, and I won't pay it."

Instead, she explains, she asked for spiritual support from the woman at the shelter.

"I simply asked her to pray with me," says Ann, her eyes brimming with tears. "I asked her, and she did. And she had heard about us, and what we were going through, and she made space for us here. And let me tell you, it's light-years better than the other shelter. My kids are safe here, I know that."

Ben knows that, but he says it still enrages him to be in the same boat with the people he dislikes.

"Like I said, there are bad people here, people I don't want my kids around. I feel like I've been taken down a notch—ten notches, I guess. It's like a doctor getting sick and finding himself in the hospital, on the wrong end of the stethoscope, you know?"

"I Don't See How We'll Make Out"

Back at the shelter the family takes the elevator up to their third-floor apartment. The apartment is four rooms: a bedroom for Ben

Ann insists that she could turn to her family for help, but she doesn't want to give them the satisfaction of knowing that she and Ben are down on their luck: "The price of asking my family is too great, and I won't pay it."

and Ann, a large bedroom with bunkbeds and shelves for the children, a bathroom, and a kitchen–living room area.

"I do like how this is set up," says Ann. "They provide your dishes, towels, flatware, toaster—everything you need. You clean this apartment, and it looks great. So many poor people, they're used to living in rat holes, you know? Even if they cleaned, it would still look like a rat hole. So after a while, they say, why clean? Here, it's a pleasure."

There is a table with family pictures, some of which bear the indelible pink stain of tear gas. Ben's prized Citizens' Award of Valor stands in the place of honor on the television. A wedding picture of Ben and Ann, in traditional Muslim dress, is displayed on another table.

"Money is tight, even for little things," says Ben. "We don't need money for food here, and that's saving us. We go over to the other building and get food to prepare here in our kitchen.

"Eventually I know we're going to get money back. I've been assured of that by the police, by people in the city. But the wheels of bureaucracy move slowly, that I know. For now we've got nothing."

Ann shrugs, and looks disgusted.

"I've been asked to come up with receipts of all the things we lost. We're supposed to make up lists, and show the proof of value," she says. "But do you know how difficult that is? How am I supposed to remember all the things we had put away, packed away in closets? You just don't organize yourself that way, at least we don't.

"I tried to tell one of the authorities that just the other day. Sure, I keep receipts for things I buy, like if I think I might be returning it. But I don't itemize everything. So even though the city says they're going to reimburse us for all this loss—the damage, the destruction, and the theft—I don't see how we'll make out."

"MAYBE AFRICA, MAYBE A FARM"

Ben says that he forces himself to look ahead. If he thinks too much about their homelessness, he becomes depressed.

"We've got to look to the future. This place is not it," he says with a frown. "I'm thinking ahead to maybe getting out of the city altogether. Maybe we can get a farm, maybe a little place within driving distance from here, but out enough to get rid of the drugs, the city problems."

Benjamin and Alice tug at his hand. "Remember about Africa," they tell him.

"Oh, yeah," Ben smiles. "Africa. We've talked some about moving there, our whole family, just going to live. It's a future plan, maybe not one we'll do in the next couple of years. But sometime, for sure. Maybe Angola, maybe Nigeria."

But Ann is not interested in this conversation. As Ben walks outside to watch the children play behind the shelter, she admits she gets impatient with her husband's dreams. She is worried about now, about what will happen when they leave the shelter. What about the children? Will this all be resolved by September when Alice and Benjamin go back to school?

"I get irritated sometimes," she confides. "I love Ben, and I agree that a farm would be nice, Africa would be exciting. But what about now? Ben isn't thinking about the fact that we've got only thirty days here at this shelter, and then we're on our own. Will we be in a park somewhere, sleeping in the bushes?

Ann obsesses about finding another home for her children, and worries that Ben doesn't take that goal seriously enough. "Ben isn't thinking about the fact that we've got only thirty days here at this shelter, and then we're on our own."

"Listen," she says, "it's hard to find a place for the five of us in a decent neighborhood. Most of the places we can afford are in crack neighborhoods, and neither Ben nor I want that again. I'm working part-time in the fall, Ben's community liaison job lost its funding, so who knows what he'll have."

Ann says that home hunting has been difficult, both because of being limited to using a bus, and because they must take their three children with them. The kids get tired pretty fast, she says.

"We had something the other day that looked really promising. An apartment building, north of town. They needed a caretaker, someone who could handle the security for the place. That would be exactly right for Ben. But then they look into our background, our rental history."

She continues sarcastically. "Gee, how do you explain that you were good tenants but that a little incident happened and our house was shot to pieces by the police? Doesn't look too great, right? So all of a sudden the people at this apartment building aren't interested in us at all. We've got nothing but dead ends."

Ben says, "Wherever we end up, I want to make sure we are a strong family. I can't imagine kids in this city growing up without two loving parents. . . . There's just too much bad stuff out there."

"That's What's Tearing the Cities Apart"

Ben has returned with the children, who are hot and tired. Benjamin turns on the television, while his sisters argue about which cartoon show to watch.

"Wherever we end up," Ben says, wearily rubbing his eyes, "I want to make sure we are a strong family. I can't imagine kids in this city growing up without two loving parents. It's hard enough with two. How can a single mother do it? There's just too much bad stuff out there.

"I want my kids to grow up away from the drugs, away from the crack and all the violence that surrounds it. I don't want to live with the crack users and dealers; I don't want to see them in the shelters. But they're a fact of life, and as long as they're running free, we're all in some degree of danger."

Ben says that if it were up to him, he'd arrest every crack dealer on the streets, and put them all in prison. Unfortunately, he knows that that just isn't possible.

"We can arrest people 24-7. That's twenty-four hours a day, seven days a week," he says. "Nothing works. It would still not lower the crime rate one bit. In this state there are 375 judges, and they have an annual caseload of over a million. So what are we going to do with these people? There are murderers, rapists, child molesters, thieves, drug users, drug sellers. Not enough space for them all in jail.

"There is so much money to be made," he says, "and that's what keeps this whole thing going. That's what we see in the black communities, now. These young kids making three thousand dollars in a week selling eight-balls of crack, they're driven around by bodyguards and chauffeurs as old as me, calling the kid 'boss.'"

Ben shakes his head in disgust.

"All these kids see that. And they say, 'Hey, man, why should I work at McDonald's flipping burgers for five dollars an hour when I can have me some of that?' It's a crime, that's what it is. That's what's tearing the cities apart, everyplace you go."

Glad to Be Muslim

Both Ben and Ann believe the solutions to such problems lie in the strength of the family and the discipline of education.

"My own passion is history," Ben smiles. "I love ancient history. I have learned that most of our people, most black Americans, came from the part of the world where Islam is the religion. It's fascinating, things you don't learn in most schools. I want my children to learn these things."

Ann agrees, and thinks schools should branch out in what they teach. Kids need to learn not only about other civilizations, she says, but also about true human values.

"I hate it," she says, "that nobody is teaching Benjamin how to really communicate with a girl. I hate the way these boys relate to girls—even boys as young as Benjamin here."

"Yeah," Ben agrees, "I don't ever want him to act like a girl is some fool, some little servant, and like he's a king. That's garbage, and we all know it. Strutting around thinking girls should be lower than him. If I ever hear him treating a girl that way, I'll come after him, and he knows it. And he won't be hitting no women, either. I'll be an old man, but I'll still be coming after him."

The need for mutual respect in a relationship and the importance of controlling one's anger are among the reasons Ben and Ann are glad to be Muslim, they say.

"We teach our kids what Muhammad says about anger," Ben says. "He taught that the furthest extent that a husband can take his anger on a woman is to touch her as though she were surrounded by a thin plate of glass. Or the furthest he can take his anger is to take three blades of grass and brush them gently on the back of her leg. I like that teaching."

"I'M HARDER ON MY KIDS THAN SOME FATHERS"

Ben willingly admits that he's stricter with his children than many fathers are, but that the way the world is forces him to be.

"I don't want my kids turning out like so many kids today. I sometimes feel that I have to be harder on them for that reason. They should be representatives of the black community, role models. I don't want them whining or complaining when things aren't easy."

Ann agrees.

"So many kids grow up screaming 'racism' when things don't go their way. Sure, there's racism. It's that kind of a world. Ben will tell you that there's police officers that call black men 'niggers' or 'boys.' And that's wrong. It's ignorant. But other than complain about it, what are you going to do about it?"

"I don't want my kids turning out like so many kids today," Ben states. "They should be representatives of the black community, role models."

"Racism is here," adds Ben, "but we don't want our children to use it as an excuse to live low lives. I want Benjamin to grow up to be a marine and after that a police officer. I'm hoping he'll want to do that—to make his community a better place, to learn discipline and pride. I don't want him to be like the rest of the trash you see out here on the street."

"THE UNFAIRNESS JUST EATS AWAY AT ME"

Even so, Ann says, her voice bristling with pent-up rage, the injustice of her family's situation sometimes seems too much for her to cope with.

"Most of the time, I'm okay," she says, "but every so often the unfairness of it all just eats away at me. I think of me and Ben going to court next week when that boy Dray goes on trial for murder. He's accused of murdering those three people in Carver County, over drugs or something, they're saying. So he's this big bad Vice Lord, a murderer. And he's in jail, getting three nice meals a day, doesn't have to worry about that.

"And hey," she continues, her voice rising in pitch, "maybe if he gets convicted of that murdering, he can take advantage of one of those nice prison programs where he can get a college degree. Go to the nice library there, use those computers. He'll be in fine shape. And here we are . . . oh, I can't tell you how mad this makes me."

Ann shakes her head and blinks back tears of fury.

"Who knows where we all will go? Who knows where we will be?"

Trina

"I'M A RECOVERING ADDICT, FOUR DAYS AGO I DELIVERED MY SIXTH CHILD, AND WE'RE HOMELESS."

At first the girl looks too young, too unsure of herself, to be babysitting the crowd of children around her all by herself. Even so, they seem to stay near her as she moves through the outer lobby of the homeless shelter. Four children stay near her legs; another dozes in a stroller. In her arms, a tiny newborn sleeps, wrapped in a stained white blanket.

Her name is Trina, and all six of these children are hers. Although she looks no more than fourteen or fifteen, she says she is twenty-two. Her eyes are heavily lidded, and she smiles nervously.

"I've had people tell me I look like a high school girl," she says with an accent that is more East Coast than Midwest. "But I'm older, I can promise you that. I've been going through some hard times, and that's a fact. I'm a recovering addict, four days ago I delivered my sixth child, and we're homeless. I guess right now it seems like things couldn't get no worse."

"I DON'T REMEMBER MUCH ABOUT BEING A KID"

While many people in this shelter are homeless for the first time, Trina says she is an old hand at it.

"My family has been homeless before," she says. "I'm not sure what it really feels like to be secure, to have a nice home that you can bring your friends to. Someplace clean and pretty—*that* would be something new for me. This shelter is no worse than any home situation I've been in, and it's a whole lot better than some of the homes I've had."

Trina grew up in New York and lived there until she was eight.

"I've been here so long that in a way it feels like I'm a native Minnesotan. I don't remember much about being a kid, of being in New York. It sort of feels like I've been this way forever, you know what I'm talking about?

"It was my mom, my older brother, and me. We were without my dad. He and my mom split up when I was real young, so she pretty much raised me. I don't have many memories of him, don't

Trina's life has been unstable since she was a small child: "We were poor, plain and simple. . . . We'd stay at a place until something happened—couldn't pay the rent or something like that. Then we'd get evicted."

have any urge to look him up, you know? He's older than my mom; I think he's living in some senior citizens' building in New York now."

"We Were Poor, Plain and Simple"

They were always poor, Trina remembers, unable sometimes even to pay their rent.

"We were poor, plain and simple," she says with a shrug. "I remember eating in the dark, sitting at home with no lights, no electricity. I guess Mom couldn't pay it, I don't really know why. But I remember eating Kentucky Fried Chicken, sitting around a box in the kitchen, not even being able to see what I was eating."

Trina pauses a moment to light a cigarette.

"You know, in some families parents might have made eating in the dark seem kind of fun, kind of an adventure, even though it was for a bad reason. But I don't think we even talked about it. It was just, 'Sit there, eat this stuff,' and that was that.

"We moved around a lot. I think we'd stay at a place until something happened—couldn't pay the rent or something like that. Then we'd get evicted. In New York they do it this way: they wait until you aren't there and they take all your stuff out of your apartment and they dump it on the curb. Tough, if it gets ripped off, you know?

"I remember coming back from school and seeing bags of stuff outside our building. People were stopping to rummage through the bags. One guy was sitting on my mom's chair, like he belonged there. I hated that they were taking stuff that was ours."

Did she say anything to those people?

"No," she says. "Maybe I was nervous about saying things to grownups; I was pretty young. I'm not sure . . . I don't know why. It was like eating chicken in the dark. It didn't seem to be important to say much about it. It was just what happened, that's all. You know what I'm saying?"

Family Violence

But poverty was only one aspect of her childhood, says Trina. There was alcoholism—her mother's—and a lot of violence.

"My parents were both alcoholics," she says. "My mom was the worst. She always was a drinker," she remembers. "She always was, since the age of sixteen, and still is. And when she drank, she'd get mean. I think she drank mostly to escape. It seemed to be more common when we were really low on money or when we were just evicted.

"My brother and her would get into huge arguments. I can remember one fight where he smashed his guitar on the bridge of her nose. I thought she died, there was so much blood. They'd do lots of yelling at each other, lots of cussing each other out. Back then I just tried staying out of the way. If they didn't see you, chances were pretty good that you wouldn't get involved in the fight."

Trina says that the drinking and the violence that accompanied it increased greatly after the family moved to Minnesota.

"My grandmother lived here," she explains. "She had passed, died, and we came out to take care of the funeral and all. She was an alcoholic, too. Anyway, we were supposed to go back to New York when the funeral and everything was taken care of, but my father called and told my mom that we'd been evicted again. Our stuff had been dumped on the curb, and this time there wasn't anything left. We didn't have anything to go back to, so I guess my mom decided we might as well stay."

ABUSE

They had no money. An aunt let the family stay with her for a little while until they could find a place to live. "That time back then was a jumble in my mind," admits Trina. "When we moved south of the city to a little apartment, my mom really got bad. Was she violent towards me? Oh, man, you don't even know. You can't even imagine it.

"Yeah, she'd be abusive all right, especially when she'd been drinking all day, since early in the morning. She'd pull me by my hair. Sometimes she'd wake me up at 3:00 in the morning and yell at me really loud, telling me to find her something to wear, that she was going out. I was sound asleep, you know, and I didn't really understand right away what she was saying to me. So I wouldn't move fast enough for her, and she'd smack me."

Trina says she was frightened, for it seemed that each time her mother went on one of these rampages it was worse than the time before.

"Sometimes you know what people's limits are," she says, without a trace of emotion. "You know that, well, they may smack you once in the face, but then they'll say they're sorry, and it will be over. But not her. You just hoped she'd stop before she killed you. I was really scared when she hit me with a big heavy frying pan, right in my face.

"I also have real clear memories of wrestling with my mom," says Trina, "trying to get a butcher knife away from her before she cut me. It's like when she slammed me with that pan. Did she mean to hurt me worse? Would she have killed me with that knife? I don't know. I don't think I want to know."

Trina's brother was abusive, too, so instead of an ally, she had another abuser to fear.

"He smacked me a lot," she says. "I had a busted lip, a broken cheekbone, stuff like that. Lots of bloody noses and swollen eyes. But it wasn't because he drank; it was because of how my mom

Trina's mother, an alcoholic, took much of her anger out on Trina. "She'd pull me by my hair. . . . You just hoped she'd stop before she killed you. I was really scared when she hit me with a big heavy frying pan, right in my face."

was when she drank. She'd say things that weren't true, or she'd exaggerate about things, making them seem worse than they really were. Then he'd get mad and start beating on me. Lots of punches, you know."

Where is her brother now?

"I'm not sure what he's doing now," she says, shaking her head slowly. "He was in jail for a while, but I think he's out now, maybe has a job somewhere. I'm not sure and I don't really care. I just hope he stays away from me, from my kids."

Taken Away

Trina says that because of her mother's drinking and the abuse she suffered, she was frequently taken out of her home by county social workers.

"My mom would start drinking, then get louder and louder. People would hear her yelling and screaming, and they'd call the police. They'd come to the house, they'd see how she was, and they'd see me. I was a little kid, so they took me to some foster home or other until she convinced them that she was sober and sorry. I guess they believed her, because I kept going back.

"I went to lots of different schools around town, though. Moving around, being in foster homes, it was hard to stay on track. I think of myself as a smart person, but I didn't learn as much as I should have in those schools. I do value education, though. I want my kids to learn what I didn't learn. I want them to read and do math. That's some time off, I know, but I think about that."

"Better Off Leaving Alone"

She began drinking when she was a sophomore in high school, says Trina.

"I've got the potential for being a chronic alcoholic," she says. "I've been told that. I suppose it's in the genes or something, because there sure are a lot of drinkers in the family. I liked how I felt when I was drunk. I didn't worry so much, and I felt a lot better off. Of course it was an escape. But if I didn't deserve an escape, I thought, who did?"

Her drinking, in addition to an uncertain and volatile home life, added to the troubles she was having in school. She was absent a great deal, and when she did go to class, she was disruptive and unwilling to listen to her teachers.

Trina had six children in seven years—by five different fathers. Many of the men Trina chose to have children with were violent to her and the children.

"I just acted like I knew everything and I didn't need to hear what anybody said," Trina remembers. "I'd rather be going out with my friends or seeing my boyfriends."

As it turned out, she says with a smile, she spent a little too much time with boyfriends. In seven years, she has had six children—by five different fathers.

"I can't say it was a mistake," she says, "because that would be disrespecting my children. It would be like saying they shouldn't be here. But I will say that most of those babies' fathers were mistakes. I got into some things I'd have been better off leaving alone."

THE BIGGEST MISTAKE OF ALL

Trina became addicted to crack when she had already had three children—one two years old, another a year old, and the third just a newborn. It was, she says, the worst time of her life.

"It was his father that got me started on crack," she says, pointing at her son Jonathan with her cigarette. "I remember I was real

Trina's drug habit interfered with her daily functioning: "I spent my whole welfare check up, spent my food stamps up, my kids were starving for something to eat. . . . I remember my kids crying at me all the time."

upset with him for bringing it around. I drank a lot but never did no drugs. I didn't want anything to do with crack.

"But then he went to jail for rape, and the friends I had that I was hanging around with were into it pretty heavy. So I did it, too. The first time I wasn't real impressed. I expected something more spectacular, I guess. It just didn't do much for me that first time. So I sure wasn't hooked after that."

It was, says Trina, after her boyfriend was released from jail and came back to her that she became an addict.

"We ended up living with his grandma," she remembers, "and that lady was a drug addict herself. Always people there, coming and going, selling it, using it. For a whole month I didn't do anything else except use crack. When I say I didn't do anything else, I'm not exaggerating. I didn't do *anything* else.

"I look back on that time and I feel real bad about it," she says. "I spent my whole welfare check up, spent my food stamps up, my kids were starving for something to eat. My hair was all over my face; I didn't brush my teeth. I don't know if I ever even changed my clothes or had a shower. I looked bad, but I couldn't care less. I remember my kids crying at me all the time, trying to climb into my lap, but I just pushed them away, told them to get away."

Trina says that her boyfriend, who was the father of two of her children, was no help, either.

"He was mean. He'd push those kids around, slam them against the wall, yell at them just for being whiny. I mean, they were hungry, you know what I'm saying? He punched me around, kicked me, used me as a punching bag. The whole thing was really sick. Even people in his family who came around punched me. I just took it—the drugs, the beating, the abuse of the kids, everything. Maybe the drugs made it easier to take, I don't know. But I know one thing: that house, his grandma's house, was a bad, bad place."

LEAVING ONE BEHIND

After a month of that, Trina says, something inside her snapped, and she knew she had to leave.

"When I said before about how I just let myself go, that was true. But there was part of me that felt bad. Not all the time, but sometimes. I knew my kids were suffering. I knew I looked bad. I saw what was happening. And so after a month of that, of me being a bad mother and him not caring about me or the kids, I got out of there. I had to.

"But they wouldn't let me take the baby, Jonathan," she says. "They wanted him to stay there, my boyfriend and his family. They had no trouble with me taking my daughter and the other boy, but Jonathan had to stay. I didn't believe that I could fight them. I'd been such a bad mother for that month I was living with them. They'd tell the authorities about my drugs and everything. I got scared and agreed to let them keep Jonathan for a time."

Trina is still angry about being forced to leave her son, and she bitterly regretted it after seeing him more than a year later.

"I got him back when he was two," she says. "I guess his father didn't want him no more. I couldn't believe it was really Jonathan. I mean, he was so stunted, so far behind where a child should be at age two. Those people hadn't been taking care of him, hadn't been feeding him anything. He was so malnourished that he couldn't even walk up steps. Just standing for any period of time was exhausting for him.

"He couldn't talk, either. He didn't even try. He was a mess, and I'll never forgive his father for what he did. I don't know why they wanted to keep him; they didn't do right by that child. What they did was evil."

UNABLE TO GO HOME AGAIN

Trina says that she tried to avoid going back to her mother's house each time a relationship failed, for she knew her mother's drinking was getting worse each year.

"She was mean; she'd yell at me, yell at the kids," says Trina. "Once she threatened to kill the baby. I can't remember what set her off that time. Sometimes when I'd be there I'd be pregnant, and that would set her off, too. She tried to get me to have an abortion, one of the times, but I wouldn't do it. I just didn't believe it was right. One time—I can't really remember when—I had an abortion, because the baby's father had beaten me so bad that the doctors didn't think the baby would come out normal.

"But otherwise, I didn't think abortion was the right answer. And adoption . . . I don't know," she says, her voice trailing off. "I just couldn't see carrying a baby for nine months and then giving him away, not knowing where he went.

"Anyway, I knew I couldn't stay long at my mother's, because things would just get worse and worse. Who knows what she'd do? I mean, I didn't doubt that she would kill one of them; she'd tried with me a few times when I was younger!"

Trina says that she really had no choice but to move home with her mother before giving birth to Lee, the newborn.

"My boyfriend and I had been staying with his mother. And that was absolutely no place for my five kids and me," she says

Although with their mother, Trina's children have suffered from an extreme level of instability, including living temporarily in the homes of Trina's mother and various boyfriends.

Having a baby and being homeless left Trina with the difficult decision of what to do with her other five children. "I knew I couldn't take them all back to the shelter with me. They only allowed one child with a mother."

firmly. "There was lots of drinking, drugs, all kinds of things that weren't healthy for my kids to be around. We tried it for a while, but it got intolerable.

"So I moved back home with the kids. I didn't really want to go back, like I said. I had to, you know? My mom didn't want me there, didn't want the kids. She hated the noise they made, especially when she was drinking, which was all the time. She didn't like the bother of them, just the bother."

NEITHER HERE NOR THERE

Shortly before Lee was born, Trina says, her mother kicked them all out of her house. Trina went into premature labor and made arrangements with a nearby children's center to care for her children while she was in the hospital.

"The people at Saint Joseph's said they'd keep my kids for a while," says Trina. "There ended up being a mixup in how long they'd keep them. I was only in the hospital for a short time—they get you in and out in twenty-four hours these days—and when I got out, I found a shelter to stay in. I called Saint Joe's to make sure my kids were okay, and they were really mad over there. They said I had left them longer than I was supposed to, and I had to go get them, or I'd lose my rights to them. I was so surprised, like I said, because I thought they were okay through the weekend."

Weak and sore from having given birth the day before, Trina went to the children's center to reclaim her five children. She says that she knew she was facing a difficult dilemma.

"I knew I couldn't take them all back to the shelter with me. They only allowed one child with a mother. The baby, Lee, I had to keep with me. And I knew I couldn't sneak five of them in there. I didn't want to leave them at my boyfriend's mother's house; I wasn't comfortable with my daughter Tracia being there, especially. And there was no way I would leave them with my mother."

The solution she came up with, she says, was to leave the boys for a few days with her boyfriend and to take six-year-old Tracia to a girlfriend's house. But even though the plan seemed a good one, it ended up in a frightening family dispute that resulted in the arrest of Trina's mother and brother.

"SHE DEMANDED CONTROL OF HER GRANDCHILDREN"

The trouble began when Trina's mother went on a two-day, non-stop drinking spree. She was angry because she didn't know where Trina and the children were, and she began calling her daughter's friends, demanding to know the whereabouts of her grandchildren.

"I knew she wouldn't know how to get in touch with my boyfriend," says Trina. "So I knew she couldn't find the boys. But then she called up my girlfriend, the one who was keeping Tracia for me. My girlfriend was scared; my mom was really frightening when she wanted to be. She was hollering and screaming about how she demanded control of her grandchildren.

"My girlfriend's mother had had a stroke recently, and she didn't want any bad business with my drunken mother coming around. Who knows what that would do to her own mother?" says Trina. "So she gave in to my mother."

What happened, Trina says, was that to avoid such "bad business" her girlfriend brought Tracia to her grandmother. When, two days later, Trina came looking for Tracia, her girlfriend told her what she had done.

"I went over to my mom's to pick up Tracia. I felt a little stronger and figured we could find a shelter where we could all be

In the confusion after the birth of her last child, Trina had to use the police to get her daughter, Tracia, back from her mother.

together. Like I said, the boys were okay at my boyfriend's for a few days, but that's all. That place wasn't good for them.

"But when I got to my mom's house, my brother was there, and he's like, 'No, there's nobody here. Tracia isn't here; we haven't seen her.' Well, I knew that was a lie. So I said to myself, here we go again. I figured, fine, I'll go get the police; they'll get Tracia out of there."

I'll Be Pressing Charges Against My Mother

The police met Trina outside her mother's house and walked with her to the door.

"They stood there with me," she remembers, "talking to my mom, listening to her lie about me. She told the police I was a bad mother, asked me why I didn't even know where my own daughter was, and can't I even keep track of her.

"The police weren't stupid. They didn't believe her. They could tell she'd been drinking. They told her to stay off the liquor, that she was out of control. They also asked permission to come into the house and have a look around, but my mom said no, that they could just get off her porch right away."

Trina accompanied the police to her girlfriend's house, to verify her story that she had left Tracia off at Trina's mother's home. Satisfied that her friend was telling the truth, the police returned to her mother's house.

"This time my brother answered the door," remembers Trina, "and he was in a mean mood, not afraid of no police. He lipped off to the police officers, then ended up punching one of them. That got him arrested. After all this, my daughter Tracia just walked right out of the house. The police arrested my mom, then, because she had been blocking my parental rights."

Trina says that she intends to press charges against her mother, and to take her to court.

"It seems real cold to do something like that, maybe, if you don't know her," admits Trina. "But I do know her, better than anybody. She's sixty-two years old and hasn't learned much in that time. My kids like her; it seems hard to believe, but they love her. They call her Grandee. She *can* be a nice person when she's not drinking. I'll admit that. But the fact is, there aren't that many times when she isn't drinking. And when she's drunk, she's so mean that she can make you forget that there's anything nice about her at all."

SHELTERS ARE NO WAY OF LIFE FOR A FAMILY

So now, with six children, a bitter feud with her family, and a boyfriend whose home is unsafe for her children, Trina is without a place to live.

"After the problems that night with my mother, I took my kids to a homeless shelter downtown, a real bad place," she says. "Everyone there is a drunk or on crack. Some are both. The shelter was for women and children only. Almost all of them were homeless because their houses had been boarded up—crack houses.

"See, there's people in this town that will pay a woman fifty bucks a day just to use her house for a little dealing. Most of the women are poor and are probably addicted to crack anyway, so they do it. And then, if the police find out and the house gets raided, the women are arrested, too. And so maybe there isn't enough evidence to throw them in jail, but they get their punishment, because all of a sudden there ain't no place for them to live, you know?

"Anyhow," she concludes, "that's who's in these shelters. Hardly anybody with any sense. The place is so dirty, and nobody acts like they care. They're no way of life for families, that's for sure. In our bathroom there was a hole in the ceiling, so when the people upstairs turned on their sink, all the dirty water—spit and filthy stuff—would come down into our bathroom. You couldn't take a bath, couldn't give your kids a bath. It was cold, too—just a sheet to cover us."

Trina says that that was a depressing time for her, and there were many times when she felt like just giving up.

"I'd just had the baby, I was tired and sore, and my kids were real needy," she says. "I couldn't go back to my mom's and I didn't want to take my kids to Saint Joseph's again. Who knows what they'd do—maybe keep them permanently, I think. So I was real nervous, real nervous."

"I DON'T KNOW WHAT'S WRONG WITH THEM"

Trina's children are impatient. They have been playing on the tiny strip of grass near the street and are bored. When the two oldest boys start wrestling, Trina loses her temper and slaps Kevin on the leg.

"I don't know what's wrong with them," she says. "Yesterday they were fighting and nearly stepped on the baby. I had him wrapped in his blanket on the grass. They could have killed him, fighting that way. Lee's so little.

"Kevin and Junior were separated when Jonathan stayed with his father for all that time, remember? Anyway, when Jonathan came home, he was two, and everything changed between him and his brother. They fight over attention, fight all the time.

"I don't know, maybe the chemistry has changed between them, or something like that. I know that the new baby is hard on the little ones, and they're all going through their own things now, with the move, having no place but a shelter. All I know is that it makes it harder on me to stay patient with them."

Trina's daughter, Tracia, is occupied with a tablet and a pen. She is drawing bears. She boasts that she is a pretty good artist and likes to color.

"They got crayons down in the day room, where the little kids go sometimes," she says. "I can draw there, and sometimes they put our pictures on the wall if they're colorful and you don't scribble out."

Her brother Terrance was pushing little Adrian in the stroller but has tired of that. Now Terrance is lying on his stomach in the grass and picks up a handful of clover. Jonathan inspects the clover and announces that Terrance has found a four-leaf clover.

"It's lucky; you should keep it," he tells Terrance.

Terrance slaps Jonathan and throws the clover in the street.

"This is the way they're being," says Trina, lighting another cigarette. "I tell them to stop it, but they just don't want to listen. I really don't know what's wrong with them."

"It's Harder for Me than Other People"

"I'm just grateful all my kids are healthy," says Trina. "All of them were five pounds or less [at birth]. I drank during all of my pregnancies, smoked. With one of them I drank a lot—way too much. I had broken up with his father and I just went on a drinking binge. He came out four pounds nine ounces, but healthy.

"Now, Lee, the baby, I was worried about. Lots of crack when I was pregnant with him, I knew they were going to find out I was on drugs when I went in to the hospital to deliver him, so before-hand I got in a chemical abuse program. I wanted to quit using anyway, and this was the best time. After all, I didn't want them to take my kids away, and they surely would have, if I was still using crack."

She has been clean and sober for a month, she says proudly.

"It's harder for me than other people, I think," she says. "I've got so much stress in my life, with being homeless and with these kids. Plus, Lee's father is in a situation where there is a lot of drinking and drugs at where he's staying, so that's hard for me, too.

"I know it's important for me to stay clean, though," she says. "But I don't want to go back to all that. I'm not going to accomplish anything being high; I understand this. We talk about that kind of thing in this group I'm in. I go every Wednesday and every Friday, and I haven't missed a meeting yet, not in a month."

"WHAT KIND OF MOTHER AM I?"

Trina will be the first to admit that she has made mistakes along the way. Her drug and alcohol use, combined with poor choices of boyfriends, have made life for her and her children difficult.

"I know how it sounds," she admits. "Really bad, that's how. The relationships were bad with the fathers of my children, I know that. Going to counseling now, being in that group, I have learned that some of my problems have stemmed from my own father not being around and my mom not being the mother she should be. Lots of bad decisions for me, doing drugs, doing things that were bad for my kids.

"I sometimes think, what kind of mother am I? I know that they say that if you are abused when you're a kid, chances are you'll abuse your own children. I have hit my kids; I admit that I do. But it was a lot worse when I was on drugs and drinking. I'm better, more patient when I'm sober and clean, that's a fact. I do the best that I can."

"MY LIFE ISN'T OVER"

With her addiction to cocaine and alcohol, her six children, her stormy relationship with her brother and mother, her uncertain relationship with her current boyfriend, is there anything in her life that is positive?

"I sometimes think, what kind of mother am I? . . . I have hit my kids; I admit that I do. But it was a lot worse when I was on drugs and drinking. I'm better, more patient when I'm sober and clean."

"My life isn't over," Trina insists. "I have a future. I'm in a self-sufficiency program called Wings. That's a good deal for me, because they help you get your education together, pay for your day care. They even pay for your transportation. They will help me set some goals for myself. That's what I need.

"I've put the Wings program on hold right now, because my chemical dependency program is top priority for me. I also have to figure out what's happening with my boyfriend, Lee's dad.

He's maybe a guy I want to stay with for the rest of my life, I don't know. But there are some changes that have to be made.

"His drinking is a real problem," she says. "It's not so much the drugs with him, because I'd have to be fair and say he does way more drinking than drugs. Right now, like I said, he's drinking a lot because of all the stress in his life."

Trina says that although some of her children's fathers have been physically abusive to her and her children, Lee's father is not like that.

"He's pretty good to me and the kids," she insists. "I mean, we've had our fights. I'm not going to say that he hasn't hit me or smacked the kids once in a while. But it's not too bad, you know? It's not like dealing with Jonathan's dad, where I could have ended up dying from the beatings. He's not bad as far as abuse."

Her counselors, however, have warned Trina that her relationship with her boyfriend could be destructive.

"They've told me that it would be hard to stay off drinking and crack if I were back with him," she says. "I understand what they're saying. But I need to do what's best, what *I* think is best, and I know him better than they do. I know he'd probably be good for us as a family."

"I Don't Like Feeling Like I'm by Myself"

But for right now, Trina says, she is on her own at the shelter with her six children. She has no immediate plans other than to continue with her chemical abuse program and to be as good a mother as she can be.

"Sometimes when I think about just giving up," she says, "I think about my mother. When I say she gives me strength, it's in a different way. Her negativism toward me makes me strong. I want to make it just to show her she's wrong about me. I'd rather be in any shelter than be back with her.

"I refuse to give her the pleasure of seeing me crawl back to her. That's what she wants me to do. She wants me to be weak, to depend on her. She doesn't want me to make it on my own. So I'm strong because of that."

Her main ambition, says Trina, is to keep custody of her children.

"I'm grateful the authorities haven't taken my kids from me," she says. "I get strength from them. I can live without the booze and the drugs, but I can't live without my kids."

Trina smiles.

"I won't say that I don't get mad at them or that I always like having kids. I don't. Sometimes I say, gee, what was I thinking? It's hard sometimes. But when they go to sleep, I look at them when they're all quiet and I say, God, I'm lucky. I don't like feeling like I'm by myself. When I'm with these six guys, I feel like I've got a whole family."

Someday, says Trina, she'd like to be established somewhere, and then this period of homelessness would feel like a bad dream.

"This kind of life I'm living now is a dead end," she says. "You know, when you're this poor, you just can't plan for anything. That's the worst part. You can't save a dollar. No plans work out, because stuff just happens to you that you can't control. Or maybe you could control it easier if you had money or a home. I don't know. There always seems to be something that happens that just ruins what you *were* going to do. That's the way it is.

"But maybe ten years from now, sometime in the future, I'd have a job. I'd be clean and sober, with no temptations. I'd like to have a car of my own and a house in a nice neighborhood."

Trina lights another cigarette and takes a deep drag.

"Mostly, I'd like to sit back and watch my kids grow up safe and happy."

Arnoldo

"TO BE HOMELESS IS CERTAINLY NOT THE WORST OF THINGS."

Arnoldo is willing to show off his home, and he is probably the only one in the world who knows it exists. It is a space within the grid pipes and cement of a large bridge near the University of Minnesota. It cannot be seen from the nearby walkways. It is not even visible if one slithers through a cyclone fence near the bridge and enters the dangerous area near the edge of the bluffs, where a misstep can send one plummeting to certain death on the rocks below.

The riverbank under the bridge is packed dirt and littered with broken glass and cigarette butts, and the cement of the bridge's base is decorated with gang slogans. People have used this part of the bridge almost certainly unaware that there is someone living directly above them.

"THIS IS MY HOME"

The room is inside the bridge, and to get to it one must climb up the large cement base to reach to the grating ten feet off the ground. This grating is the floor of Arnoldo's home; his ten-foot-high ceiling is actually the roadbed over which the semis and cars thunder day and night.

Arnoldo's home is mostly sleeping area, separated from the rest of the space by a sheet of plastic suspended from the ceiling. The bottom of the plastic is held in place by several jugs of water. A little bag containing toothpaste and toothbrush sits in one corner, next to a canvas bag with a stack of clean, folded laundry. The bed has no mattress but, rather, is composed of several colorful

Arnoldo reads in the comfort of his home under the bridge. "For now, this suits my needs perfectly. I'm very happy here."

blankets and an open sleeping bag. A small flashlight hangs by a string over his bed, and several books are stacked nearby.

"This is my home," says Arnoldo, an immensely likable thirty-four-year-old man from Guatemala. "I've lived here for several months, and hopefully I'll be here a few more. The winters get awfully cold here, so by the end of October, I know I'll be making other plans. For now, though, this suits my needs perfectly. I'm very happy here."

"THIS IS A BIG IMPROVEMENT"

Arnoldo is small and lean, with dark hair and a thick moustache. He wears a navy-blue baseball cap with the University of Minnesota *M* on it—a valuable find in the student union after the school term was over.

"It was sitting there, had been there a few days. I kept my eye on it when I came through there," he smiles. "I figured after that time nobody was going to claim it, and I sure needed a cap."

His clothes are clean and neat—a white T-shirt and khaki shorts. He has recently done his laundry, he says.

"I know many homeless people do not bathe, do not wash their clothes," he says. "They often sleep in their clothes. I myself have done that plenty of times. But I am a person who likes being clean. I must have my shower, my hair must be clean. I don't like not brushing my teeth. So my daily routine includes doing these things."

"The most important thing my father did for me was to give me pride in who I was. He gave me the freedom to choose the direction of my life."

Arnoldo has been homeless for a good deal of his adult life, although he insists his background makes him unlike many homeless people in this city.

"I am from an upper-middle-class family in Guatemala," he explains. "I know what it is like to live with money. I have spent time with my grandparents in their elegant home, with seven maids to do all the unpleasant work. I have seen profound wealth and was quite comfortable in those situations. But I have seen horrible, terrible things, too, things that I cannot erase from my mind even now, years later."

Arnoldo smiles sadly.

"But this," he says, motioning around his home in the bridge, "is certainly not the worst of things. To be homeless, here in this bridge, with books and privacy and quiet, this is a big improvement in my life."

A STRONG FAMILY BACKGROUND

Arnoldo speaks warmly of his family and his childhood. "We lived in Guatemala City, the capital of Guatemala," he says. "My family valued education and instilled that in me. My mother was a nurse; my grandfather had taught mathematics at the University of San Carlos in Guatemala."

It is his father that Arnoldo speaks of with special fondness, however. His father, he says, influenced him more than any other person in his life.

"He had a degree in accounting," says Arnoldo, "but he chose to become a tour conductor. He was very, very intelligent. He knew eight different languages, which is what made him so good at his work. He could converse with anyone.

"The most important thing my father did for me was to give me pride in who I was," he says quietly. "He gave me the freedom to choose the direction of my life. Part of that choice involved a pride in who I was, what my heritage was."

"IN HER MIND, THE MAYAN PEOPLE WERE DIRT"

"Like many Guatemalans," he says, "I am a mixture of Spanish and Mayan—the people indigenous [native] to Guatemala. And in my country, although the Mayan people are the majority—85 or 90 percent—they are the ones most enslaved. They are the lowest class of people.

"My father was very, very aware of what was going on with the Mayan people. Although we were a mixture of Mayan and Spanish, he gave me pride in that Mayan part. That Mayan part was denied by many people in my family."

Arnoldo says that he and his sister would stay occasionally with his grandparents, who lived in a large mansion in the city.

"They had maids working from 4:00 in the morning until midnight," he says, "cooking, cleaning, washing. There were more rooms in that house than I could count, I think. The maids were Mayan, of course, since no one of Spanish descent would do such work in Guatemala.

"But as hard as they worked, my grandmother was abusive to them, calling them names, yelling at them when they didn't work quickly enough. That was what one could do to Mayan people; it was done all the time. My father would argue with her. He'd say, 'What are you doing, we are all Mayans!' But she wouldn't listen. In her mind, the Mayan people were dirt that she could stand on whenever she chose."

A Dangerous Occupation

Arnoldo graduated from the University of San Carlos with a degree in political science. His goal, he says, was to work for the equality of the Mayan people in Guatemala.

"I became a labor organizer," he says. "I knew that was one important way to help. By working for better wages for Guatemala's workers, better living conditions, I could make a contribution to the people of my country."

Arnoldo admits now that although he was very enthusiastic, his expectations were too high. He did not realize, he says, how difficult and dangerous the occupation of labor organizer could be.

"The pay of the workers was very, very low—far lower than any American would even dream of working for. And the people were mistreated on the job. The conditions in the factories and plants were intolerable. So, it was not terribly difficult to organize people to have a sit-in or to strike.

"However, what we were doing was really dangerous. It is hard to imagine, living in America, where workers are allowed to protest their wages. In Guatemala, it was all right that there was a union, an organization of workers. And it was all right that I was paid by that union to help them. But our activities were closely monitored by the government's security forces.

"The government did not want the workers to be powerful, for that lessened the government's power, they thought. So the Mobile Military Police were often called in to physically force workers back on the job."

We Made a Pact Between Us

Arnoldo says that it was not uncommon for the police to shoot at striking workers or for organizers to be kidnapped and later killed.

"It happened with people I worked with," he says. "Twenty-eight organizers I worked with were having a staff meeting, and armored vans and cars burst into the building and seized them. We feared the worst, and later we found out we were correct. Two of them were found in a ditch a couple of weeks later. The corpses were almost unrecognizable, with tongues and eyes cut out, distinguishing marks like tattoos cut off, fingernails pulled away. These were not only signs of torture, but ways the government had of masking their victims' identities."

It was because of such hazards, he says, that he and his coworkers created a system by which they could identify one another.

"We all had some little tattoo put on," he explains. "Something the military police would not even notice, but something we would look for. Mine is a little blue dot by my right knee. One woman had a tiny star tattooed under her arm."

Such grisly precautions were reminders that murder and torture were a fact of life, says Arnoldo, that labor organizers had to come to terms with. It was a fact that he himself experienced—a time of his life that still gives him nightmares.

Enduring the Treatments

Arnoldo was awakened by military security police at 6:00 one morning, and told he must accompany them to their headquarters. They wanted information about labor activities and other organizers, and as soon as Arnoldo could help them, they promised, he would be released. What followed were forty-eight days of torture and horrible physical abuse, a time during which he felt he would surely die.

"They called the interrogation sessions with me treatments," he says quietly. "I didn't really know what to expect, you know? The first day they fed me breakfast, tried to make me feel comfortable. I had refried beans, milk, a little bread, some coffee. I had started to relax and thought maybe they just *did* want to talk.

"Then they came in with the hood—a rubber inner tube, sewn together on one end, the other end open. Inside it was packed with powdered fertilizer. One of the men put my hands together in handcuffs behind my back. Two others stood in front of me; one of them karate kicked me in the stomach. I lost air, and at that moment, they put the hood on. I couldn't breathe; the fertilizer was choking me. It felt like my face would shatter, and my lungs would soon explode."

Arnoldo said that he vomited, and as they continued to kick him in the stomach, he lost control of his body, defecating and urinating in his clothes.

In Guatemala, Arnoldo saw people he worked with killed by the secret police: "The corpses were almost unrecognizable, with tongues and eyes cut out, distinguishing marks like tattoos cut off, fingernails pulled away."

"I had no power," he says. "They were totally in control of me, at least of my body. My mind and my will, however, were my own. These police wanted me to sign a paper saying I was a Communist and I was working against the Guatemalan government. But that was not true. I wouldn't sign that paper, wouldn't talk about my fellow organizers."

SURVIVING

It was not that he was a hero, says Arnoldo, or that he had more strength than other people. It was simply that he had made a commitment to his friends, and he knew he had to keep it.

"My father was fighting a battle with cancer at this time," says Arnoldo. "He was a young man—only fifty-four when he died. And even though he was feeling bad, the two of us would have long talks about loyalty. Like I said, he had strong ideals and wanted me to be the same.

"My father would say, 'I have a commitment to your mother, and I will honor it until I die. We have gone through hard times and good times together. When you make a commitment, Arnoldo, never hesitate, even if you have to lose your life in the process. Don't hesitate. Because, if you duck a fight, if you pass up your chance to do the honorable thing, to honor your commitment, your life will be much harder.'

"So as things were frightening and I was in pain, I knew I had to honor that commitment. My father would be proud of me, I thought to myself. It is true that an individual can do amazing things when someone believes in him."

Arnoldo says that the treatments varied, from sessions with the hood to beatings to long periods of solitary confinement in a jungle cell.

"They sliced my belly with razors," he says, showing the scars, "just deep enough to draw blood. Then they would pour lemon juice and salt in the wounds. Or they would twist rubber bands around and around my fingers to cut off the circulation, and then beat my fingertips with a wooden ruler." In one particularly painful treatment, they would wire him to an electric box that would deliver shocks via wires that were attached to his mouth, his ears, and his testicles, as his captors asked him questions.

"The last thing was the worst. I still have trouble thinking about it. They said they wanted to show me something. They brought in some young people—men, women—who they already had decided would be killed. They raped the women, hurt them, tortured them. And they cut these people, hacked at them with machetes. These were people that were helping organize the farmworkers of Guatemala.

"I was sick; it was too much for me," Arnoldo says softly. "I still didn't sign the confession they wanted me to sign, and I did not talk about the whereabouts of other organizers. But I think something died inside me then."

Getting Out

It was pure luck that allowed Arnoldo to be released from his cell. His brother-in-law, who had always aspired to Guatemalan politics, was elected as a congressman from one of the districts.

"He and I did not agree on many things. He was further to the right of me politically, but he is a good man," says Arnoldo. "He had some contact with military people in the government and said, "If Arnoldo is alive, please return him." He couldn't get any more involved than that, because he didn't want to risk his life, or the life of my sister. But that was what freed me. After forty-eight days of the treatments, I was dumped three blocks from my mother's house."

His mother didn't recognize him and thought he was a panhandler. It was his sister who knew him and started to cry.

"I looked awful," he says. "My normal weight was about 160, and I had dropped to 80 pounds. I looked like a concentration camp survivor. I was dirty, with filthy hair. They had given me clothes that were far too big for me, and I had no shoes.

"My mother almost fainted when she realized who I was. She took me into a shower and bathed me. I was too weak to do it myself. She took care of my wounds and hooked me up to IVs with vitamins. In a few days I was feeling a little stronger, although I still looked like a skeleton for months."

It Was Then That My Homelessness Began

As soon as Arnoldo began to regain a little strength, his brother-in-law advised him to leave Guatemala.

"He said that it was not safe for me there, and that the next time I was seized it would be the end," says Arnoldo. "He asked me where I wanted to go, and I thought that Mexico would be good. He gave me some money and said he'd help me leave."

Arnoldo decided to cross the border first into Belize, a small British colony to the east of Guatemala, where a lot of Mayan people lived. Later he would go west into Mexico.

"It was the beginning of my homelessness," Arnoldo says. "I did not know where I would go, what would happen to me. And how could I know what helpful people I would meet along the way?"

Arnoldo was resting on a city bench in Belize when he was approached by a man and his wife. They recognized him as Guatemalan and offered to help him.

Arnoldo was also arrested by the Guatemalan secret police: "They sliced my belly with razors, just deep enough to draw blood. Then they would pour lemon juice and salt in the wounds."

"The man was a bishop of a district of Belize," says Arnoldo. "He and his wife could tell I was sad, somehow. I'm not certain how they knew, but they said they just knew I was going through something very difficult.

"It is hard to say this," says Arnoldo, "but when they acted so concerned for me, I did something I do not usually do: I cried. I cried for a long time, and told them my story. I just broke down, and they just listened.

"After we talked, they invited me to come to their village, deep in the jungle of Belize. I could stay there as long as I wanted, they said, until I was healthy. I agreed, and we set off for their village."

At first he simply rested, sleeping long hours and eating good food, which the church members prepared for him.

"It was good for my body, good for my heart, I think," says Arnoldo. "I had time to think about things, to meditate. After I was stronger, the people there got me a job in the village as a mechanic. I was happy working among the Mayan people."

Danger in Mexico

After nine months Arnoldo decided it was time to go. He wanted to go to Mexico City, hoping to meet up with more Guatemalans who had fled as he had. However, his welcome in Mexico was not as warm as it had been in Belize.

"I met up with some people right away, right after I crossed into Mexico," he says. "They said, 'No, don't even think about staying here. Mexico is dangerous for Guatemalans and people from El Salvador right now.'

"They told me that an organization called the White Hand was rounding up people who had fled El Salvador and Guatemala. This organization sent the people back across the border to their countries. What was worse, if they found out that the people were criminals or were wanted by those governments, the White Hand would kill them on the spot, right there in Mexico."

Deciding Mexico was not for him, Arnoldo resolved to go north across the Rio Grande into Texas. He admits that the United States was never on his list of countries to visit.

"I want to be really honest with you," he says, smiling with a hint of embarrassment. "I never really wanted to come to the United States. It was not in my mind, you know? In a way, I saw this country as the enemy, because it has been supporting my government—the very people who were murdering indigenous Guatemalans! In fact, many people in my country believe that the reason we are as restricted as we are is because the United States wants to keep the status quo.

"It is nothing personal against the people of this country, you understand. There is a lot here that I love, many people who have been good to me. But that is the feeling I had about the government of this country, anyway."

INTO THE UNITED STATES

However, crossing the border into the United States proved to be more of a problem than he expected.

"I knew I didn't dare swim the river," he said, "because I'm not that strong a swimmer. I stayed by the riverbank for a few nights, thinking about what I should do, when one night I heard trucks coming. At first, I thought they were immigration officers looking for people like me. But then, when they turned off their lights and began talking on walkie-talkies, I knew just what they were—drug smugglers!"

Arnoldo watched them uncover a well-hidden boat near the shore and make a trip back and forth in the dark. When they finished their business and drove away in their trucks, he found the boat and used it to get across the river.

"If I'd had any doubts what they were doing before, I sure didn't have them after looking at the boat," he says, laughing. "There, in the bottom, was a big chunk of marijuana! I thought, wow, here is my money for the rest of the trip! I have used marijuana before, and I was not worried about selling a little of it for money."

Arnoldo smiles.

"I don't want to lie, you know."

"WE HAVE A SPECIAL PLACE FOR YOU GUYS"

Once he crossed the border into Texas, Arnoldo had some trouble. He had been advised to stay off the roads. He had been given directions that would take him to a town where he could find food and lodging. But he became hopelessly lost.

"I found myself walking in big circles around and around the desert," he says. "By the sixth day of doing this, I was exhausted, hungry, and discouraged. I'd drunk water from cattle ponds—

anything to quench my thirst. I finally told myself, I'm going to take the first road I see; I don't care where it leads. I don't care if it leads right to the headquarters of the border patrol!

"So I did, and within five minutes I had three border patrol cars around me." He laughs. "I was going to tell them I was Mexican so they would just dump me back across the border. But one of them said, 'You don't look Mexican. Tell the truth—are you from Guatemala or El Salvador?'

"I told them the truth, and boy, was I surprised. They told me, 'We have a special place for you guys, since you are fleeing political persecution.' They said I had a right to an attorney and that they would be taking me to a camp where I would be safe for the time being."

Arnoldo was taken to a refugee center that was mainly for people fleeing from Central American countries and seeking political asylum. He stayed there for three months until his lawyer was able to secure papers and a work permit for him.

"She told me, 'This afternoon you're going to be free, so decide what you want to do, where you want to go.' She said that from now on, I could move about how I wanted to in the United States. She told me she was sure I'd be okay."

"I'D PUT MY FINGER RIGHT ON DES MOINES"

When he left the camp, Arnoldo spent time in San Antonio and Dallas but did not feel that either one of those places was right for him. He was eager to see more of the United States and one day took out a map.

"My friends gathered around, and I told them I was going to leave it to chance," he remembers with a smile. "I closed my eyes and stuck my finger down. When I looked, I saw that I'd put my finger right on Des Moines, Iowa!"

He had no idea what to expect, knowing only that he was free to travel. Hitchhiking, he found, was a pleasurable experience.

"Everyone was so friendly," he says. "I wasn't nervous anymore about telling people where I was from, so that helped me relax. But people were generous and kind—especially the truck drivers. It took me about four days to reach the city."

On his last ride a large blond man picked him up in Kansas. His name, says Arnoldo, was Father Jim, a Jesuit priest who, by strange coincidence, had lived in Guatemala for twenty-two years.

Arnoldo was able to enter the country legally, because the United States had granted asylum to Guatemalan political prisoners. He says, "From now on, I could move about how I wanted to in the United States.

Like Arnoldo, Father Jim had been considered a danger to the Guatemalan government for his work with the poor. Now he lived in Milwaukee, Wisconsin, and ran a refugee center for Guatemalans and El Salvadorans who had fled to the United States.

"He offered to help me," says Arnoldo, "and that's what he did. He introduced me to the bishop of Des Moines, who let me stay in his home until I found work. The bishop told me about a Catholic shelter in the city that helped homeless people. Would I like a job helping out there, he asked?"

Arnoldo shakes his head in wonderment.

"Imagine!" he says. "Within a few days of coming to this strange city, I not only had a job, I was on friendly terms with the bishop!"

"I FELT AT HOME WITH THEM"

For more than a year Arnoldo worked in the shelter in Des Moines. He cleaned rooms, cooked, and even helped scavenge local supermarket dumpsters for usable food for the shelter kitchen. In return he received a small salary, a room of his own, and free meals.

"I enjoyed it all," he says. "I feel a great bond with the homeless—a way no one but another who has been homeless himself can feel. When I was with the families that came to the shelter, or with the single men who came, I felt at home with them."

Only after falling in love with a girl from Minneapolis did he think about leaving. His friends at the shelter advised him to stay.

"Her name was Pamela," says Arnoldo, "and she wanted me to come back to Minneapolis with her. It seemed as though we could be happy, and it had been so long since I had had a relationship with someone.

"The staff at the shelter rolled their eyes at me. They said they thought it would be a mistake, that I hardly knew this girl. But in the end, when I told them it was a hard decision, but I was going with Pamela to Minneapolis, then they told me that there would always be a place for me there [at the shelter]."

Unfortunately, he says, the relationship with Pamela did not work out. After several months of living together, Pamela became a born-again Christian, and her lifestyle changed dramatically.

"It was like night and day," says Arnoldo. "All of a sudden she became someone I didn't know. And her new pastor told me it was best if I left. He said marriages between white people and people 'like me' could never work. So I left. And once again I was homeless."

LIVING IN THE PARK

Arnoldo says that although he'd been homeless before, it was the first time he'd ever had to fend for himself in a big American city.

Arnoldo sits in the park where he sometimes spends his days reading. He attempted to live in the park when he first became homeless.

"At first I wondered if I should go back to Des Moines or call Father Jim in Milwaukee. He'd always said that if things didn't work out, I should call and he'd send me bus fare.

"But I just couldn't make myself do either one of those things, you know? It had been four or five months since Des Moines, and more than a year since I'd seen Father Jim. I felt that to seek their help would be embarrassing and discourteous. I didn't want them to know what mistakes I had made with my life, I think."

So Arnoldo ended up on the streets of Minneapolis. At first he knew nothing about shelters available in that city, so he spent his nights in a city park.

"Back then the police weren't eager to round up homeless people and take them to the shelters, as they are now," he says. "They'd let you sleep outside, provided you didn't make disturbances drinking or doing drugs.

"My life was fairly routine then. I took my meals in a place called the Branch, run by local churches. I didn't like to sit inside the Branch all day drinking coffee, like some people do, so I'd go to the library and hang out. I like to read—almost anything is interesting to me—and I found this a pleasant way to pass the time.

"In fact, I even got a library card during that time," he laughs. "I asked the woman at the library if I could give the address of the Branch as my residence, and she said, 'Why not?' So I took out books, took them back to the park, and read on nice days.

"I didn't sleep right in the park; instead, I had stashed an old quilt in some bushes in a vacant lot behind the park. I also stashed a backpack with two changes of clothes and underwear.

"It was actually kind of nice living that way," he says. "Really quiet, no one bothered me. But later, I found out why it was so quiet, why no other homeless people were trying to steal my spot in the park. A Mexican guy at the Branch explained it to me—the other homeless men were all in shelters!"

"I Missed the Shelter"

The Mexican man Arnoldo talked to urged him to go to a shelter, especially since autumn was quickly approaching.

"He asked me if I had ever seen snow; I told him a little back in Des Moines, but not too much. He laughed and told me, wait until you see what winter in Minnesota is like. So he told me about a shelter called Saint Stephen's and told me to come along with him there.

"The people who ran the place were very nice," says Arnoldo. "It reminded me a lot of the shelter in Des Moines. I found a job as a cook at a country club near Lake Calhoun and started making some money. The staff let me stay there, since I was saving up for a place to live.

"It's funny," he says, "but as soon as I got my money together and got my apartment, I missed the shelter. I missed the people, missed the feeling of being around people who had stories to tell. So after work at the country club, I came downtown and volunteered at the shelter. I brought food I'd cooked at the restaurant and gave it to the people. I was feeling much better about things."

After six months of volunteering at Saint Stephen's after work, Arnoldo was offered a staff position. When he realized he would be making about the same salary as he was making as a cook, he took the job.

"It felt good to be back again, working and living with the homeless people," he admits. "I was useful, since I could speak both Spanish and English. It was where I wanted to be."

MARRIAGE AND MISTAKES

It was while he was on staff at the shelter that he met a young college student named Samara. She was ready to graduate with a degree in theology, and had a real interest in justice issues in Central American countries.

"We got along very well," says Arnoldo, "and we gradually fell in love. Samara and I got married—an event that had both terrible and wonderful results."

Arnoldo quit his job at the shelter and found another job as a cook in a restaurant. Samara got a job teaching at a nearby university. When she became pregnant, they were both happy, hoping that a baby might help strengthen their marriage.

"It was exciting to think about a baby coming," he says, "even though we weren't getting along too well then. I cannot say exactly what it was, but neither of us was happy. Anyway, it was decided that I would stay home and be a househusband when the baby was born, and Samara would resume her job at the university."

Arnoldo says that the birth of their daughter, Maya, was thrilling.

"She was so beautiful," he says, "blonde and big eyed. You look at this little person, and you think, my God, this girl can do anything; her whole life is ahead. But the one thing a baby cannot do, of course, is fix a marriage that isn't meant to be."

The breakup occurred because of what he calls "a stupid act of unfaithfulness" on his part.

"It was very wrong of me," he says, "and I went to her and begged forgiveness. I don't know if she would have ever found out otherwise, but it was a burden I didn't want to carry any longer. She was angry, and the next day she told me to leave the house and never come back. I left immediately, taking nothing but the clothes on my back.

"I was very upset, very sad. It was for Maya that I grieved, for one minute I was in her life, the next I was gone. That was traumatic, I am sure. Anyway, I was homeless again, and for the first two weeks I didn't do nearly as well as I had done as a homeless man in the past."

"ALL I DID WAS DRINK, SMOKE, WALK"

Arnoldo says that he was so upset at first that he could think of nothing to do except lose himself.

"I went into a bar and drank. I got very, very drunk," he says. "I walked that night, back and forth along the river. I walked from the university all the way to Saint Paul, to the Ford Bridge. I don't even know what I thought about, or if I thought at all. I just walked—twenty-five miles that night!

"That's kind of what I did for the first three weeks. I didn't want to go to sleep; I could not. I bought a twelve-pack of beer every night and stashed it in some bushes by the river, and walked all night, or sat in the park. Sometimes I walked south of the city and bought some marijuana and smoked that. All I did was drink, smoke, and walk. I looked awful, I smelled awful, but I didn't care."

Arnoldo's downward spiral stopped when he went into a university law library one morning to use the bathroom.

"I saw these students just sacked out, sleeping on couches there. I thought to myself, that is what I need. It is hard to explain; it looked so inviting, so cool. So I called Samara and asked her to bring me a change of clothes. She agreed, and I went to the river and washed, changed my clothes. I went back to that law library, found myself one of those nice leather couches, and went to sleep—for fourteen hours straight."

Arnoldo says that when he woke up, his head was clear, and he realized he needed to get on with his life.

"I wasn't going to drink like that, or smoke marijuana," he says. "I wanted to go back on track, you know? I wanted to find a shelter because it was starting to get cold again, and I wanted to do this with a clean mind, a clean start."

Arnoldo obtained a library card, and reads heavily.

Unwelcome Suggestions

Arnoldo spent that winter in a shelter called Our Savior's. After a while the staff asked him if he would like to work there, and he agreed.

"It never really worked out," he says. "They told me that they wanted to reorganize, to make some changes in the way the shelter worked. They asked me what I thought, and I told them. That was my big mistake, I think.

"I told them that too many drunks were being admitted to the shelter, that they were abusive to some of the workers and the other homeless people. I told them how one of the staff members was using crack and was selling it to some of the residents in exchange for sexual favors. I told them about one staff guy who was having sex with a homeless woman, a woman who had some mental problems. This wasn't right, I said, and I told them they should fire those guys."

The senior staff members of the shelter were reluctant to make the changes Arnoldo suggested, however.

"They worried about being too strict," he complains. "They thought it would be bad if some people were turned away from the shelter, since these were the people that needed the most help.

"As for the abuses of the staff, they didn't want to fire people without proof. I guess I understand that, but I was telling them things I knew because I had been on the other side, you know? I'd been a resident, I'd seen the things happening that they didn't see, after they'd gone home for the night.

"After our meetings things changed between me and the staff," he says. "I am not someone they like. They decided they no longer wanted me as a staff person, and *I* decided that I was no longer welcome as a resident, either. That is best, I think."

A Routine Life on the Streets

Today, says Arnoldo, he is quite happy with his home in the bridge.

"I found it by accident," he says, smiling. "I was walking by and saw the broken fence. When I went through the fence and investigated, I could really see the possibilities.

"The only drawback is that the walkways are busy, and it's hard for me to slip inside the fence before about 1:00 in the morning. There are students, police, people driving by, walking by. And I don't want to be seen; I don't want trouble."

His life has once again taken on the forced routine of a homeless person in a city, he says.

"I get up at about 9:00, walk over to one of the university buildings where there is a bathroom and brush my teeth and take care of my personal business," he explains. "Once I'm done there, I walk over to the Branch to have breakfast. If I need to do some laundry or take a shower, I get up earlier. You have to do that, because there are only a few washing machines, and they get busy fast."

Arnoldo says that he knows a few homeless people at the Branch but tends to stay to himself, not talking much.

"I am not unfriendly," he explains, "but I do not wish to get caught up in other people's battles. Some of them are so angry, almost psychotic. I don't want to hear about how they're going to get someone who crossed them or what they're going to do with their girlfriends, you know? Once in a while there will be some people who enjoy talking about politics, things like that.

"I do a lot of walking. I visit the libraries and continue to check out books. I eat my dinner at the Branch and maybe hang around by the river at a park or something before I head back to my bridge."

MAKING MONEY

Arnoldo is not able to get a job, for his work permit has expired, a fact that worries him greatly.

Arnoldo has a few friends at the Branch, where he eats his meals with other homeless people, but does not get too close to any one of them. "I do not wish to get caught up in other people's battles. Some of them are so angry, almost psychotic."

"I'm supposed to be able to renew my permit every year," he says. "That's the way it has always been. It is illegal for me to work without a permit, and it is illegal for someone to hire me without it. But the last time I tried to renew it, I was turned down.

"They told me that my file is now in Omaha, and I had to send things to that office. Then, when I wrote to Omaha they said that I had to go through the immigration office in Virginia. It has never been this difficult, and I am nervous. Especially because I have been outspoken in my criticism of the way the U.S. government is backing the military in Guatemala. Once, back when I was working at the shelter, a newspaper guy even interviewed me about

Arnoldo climbs through the fence to enter his home under the bridge. He prefers the bridge to the homeless shelters.

that. It was probably not wise to talk like that. But maybe I'm being paranoid. Maybe this has nothing to do with my work permit, I don't know."

For now, Arnoldo says, he makes a little money being an interpreter for the Latino people at the Branch.

"Sometimes someone wants to sell something—a radio or a Walkman or something," he explains. "That happens a lot when people are evicted and need fast cash. Or maybe someone needs to go to the welfare office or the hospital or something and doesn't speak English. They'll pay me a little money to help them with the forms or something.

"Once in a while, I'll be a go-between for a Latino who wants to buy drugs," he admits. "I won't buy the drugs or go along when they do it, but I'll arrange a time or help them find out the price or something."

THE SHELTERS ARE TOO VIOLENT

One aspect of homelessness he has learned is to avoid the shelters. In the last year shelters for single men have become dangerous places.

"They are simply too violent," he says, shaking his head in disgust. "I'll never go back to a shelter. One of the biggest ones in town is called the Drake. I've tried it. There are twelve men to a room, and that's bad. You stay awake all night, just making sure people aren't stealing your shoes or going through your pockets.

"Police officers sit downstairs, but even with them there, people are coming and going all night, banging doors, shouting, drunk. The last night I was there, there were two guys going door to door, selling crack. I mean, they have rules, but no one enforces them, no one cares."

Arnoldo admits that it is not just the shelters but the streets around the shelters that have added to the violence. There are many young black kids, he says, who go after Latinos.

"I was chased down last week," he says incredulously, "by a gang of black kids on bicycles. I mean, they were *kids*—the youngest was about seven. But they were carrying pipes and raggedy pieces of metal, and they hit me on the back."

He shows four ugly-looking red marks on his middle back.

"It doesn't hurt much, and it isn't so bad now, but it really scared me. I know they're just kids, and they don't know better, but I get angry sometimes. I think about how I wish some of these tough kids who think they're so macho could get a few minutes in a Guatemalan police station."

He laughs. "They'd be crying for their mothers. I've seen grown men do that."

"I Have Heard Rumors"

Arnoldo says he is generally a cheerful man and that very few things annoy or depress him.

"There are two things that eat away at me," he says. "I have gotten word that there may be trouble for my family in Guatemala. My brother-in-law recently switched parties. He is now further to the left, a fact which has angered many of the people in his old party.

"I have heard rumors that my sister and my mother may have been murdered," he says, his brown eyes filling suddenly with tears. "I don't know this to be a fact, but it seems possible. In my heart, I guess I am ready for that news. I believe it has happened.

"The other sad thing for me is my daughter Maya," he says. "She is now five years old. I have not seen her since last January. Samara is very hurt still by my betrayal of her. She will not let me see Maya for more than a few minutes each time.

"I have not wanted to put Maya in the position that so many other children are in today," he says. "I will not use her in a custody fight. That would be mean. I would not hurt her that way. Samara is not ready to talk to me yet. I told her I will wait. If it takes five more years, or ten, I will wait. I want to be Maya's father, you see."

Not There, Not Here

For the time being Arnoldo is very content with the state of his life, although he knows that with the onset of colder weather his days under the bridge may be numbered.

"I may try to find a shelter that I can stay in without being in danger," he says, "or I might move on. I hate to go too far from here, since Maya is in this city, and I enjoy even a few minutes with her. But I guess we'll see. Maybe Seattle will be warmer than here, just for the winter. I've heard that it is milder on the West Coast.

Arnoldo holds a picture of his daughter, Maya, whom he now rarely sees.

"I feel like I'm between things right now. I have no news about my work permit. I have no news about my family in Guatemala. I have no news about my status with Maya.

"I have been away from Guatemala for more than ten years," he says slowly, "and so I know I have lost my citizenship. I am not there, I am not here, you know? I'm not sure where I really am."

"I'LL SURVIVE"

Religion is not a big factor in Arnoldo's life, although he was brought up Roman Catholic.

"I learned tai chi when I was a young man in Guatemala," he says. "A bunch of my friends and I even had a tai chi master who taught us some of the self-defense moves. But mostly I like the chants and the idea that there are many gods, many positive forces watching over us. I chant in the morning; that helps me get balanced and clearheaded. And I bow when I come home to my bridge and when I am about to leave it. That shows respect for my home, for the gods."

The discipline and humanity he gets from his practice of tai chi would be good for many people, he says, especially those who deal with the homeless.

"I think that's one of the big problems in shelters, in places like the Branch. People think all homeless people are the same, and that isn't right. Not all of us are drunks, or drug addicts. Many are not criminals, are not dangerous in any way. So why do these people who deal with us act as if we were?

"No matter what happens, I'll survive. Nothing can happen to me that's as bad as what's already happened."

"I'll give you an example," he says. "Yesterday I wanted to do laundry, so I got up at 6:30 in the morning to get to the Branch, to put my name on the waiting list. I was first in line. I was really happy.

"So I'm doing my laundry, I had a shower, I'm feeling great. Then this other homeless guy comes in—didn't know the system—and started taking my stuff out of the washers and loading his stuff in. I told him not to, and he got mad, started shouting. But I kept talking to him, explaining how it all worked, and he started to listen.

"But just then, this woman who just started working there at the Branch comes over because she heard the yelling. She took us by the collars and said, 'You two—OUT!' Like we were just trash. I tried to explain that we had everything under control, but she wouldn't listen. Nobody takes time to listen. So no laundry gets done, nothing gets resolved. That guy and I both walk away mad. Man, I hate that stuff, I just hate that."

Arnoldo smiles again.

"Anyway, I shouldn't complain," he says. "I've got clean clothes now, and I had a shower this morning. I'm better off than a lot of these guys, because I've got a nice quiet place to live, nobody hassling me.

"The police around here don't exactly know I live here, but I think they trust me; they say hello and wave. I'm a regular in the park. They aren't worried about me."

As though on cue, a black-and-white police car cruises slowly by the park. A ruddy-faced officer waves at Arnoldo, who waves back.

"See what I mean?" he says. "No matter what happens, I'll survive. Nothing can happen to me that's as bad as what's already happened. I'll survive."

Epilogue

Since the four people in *The Other America: The Homeless* was written, a number of changes have occurred which readers will no doubt find interesting.

Trina, the young mother of six who was so proud of being clean and sober for one month, started drinking again. Workers at the shelter say that she was told to leave after breaking several of the shelter rules—namely, drinking on the premises and having a man in her room.

Ann and Ben used up their thirty days in the shelter, and are now living in a car. Ann says she is incredulous that the city has not repaid them for their loss yet, and she mourns the coming of fall, for as she says, "School is starting, and my kids have no home, nowhere to come home to."

Marilyn is living temporarily with her daughter Lisa, although the two agree that the arrangement cannot be permanent. Her health continues to fail, and she says that she has days when it is difficult for her to organize even the smallest tasks for herself.

There is also a change in the life of Arnoldo, who came to the United States as a political refugee from Guatemala. Late in the summer, workers repairing an Internet cable discovered Arnoldo's bridge home, and forced him to leave. He tried moving into a shelter, although he had had no luck with shelters before. This one, however, is quite different—says Arnoldo, "the people are wonderful." Some have offered to help him get his work permit renewed, which would give him far more options at living arrangements. Arnoldo smiles and shrugs his shoulders. "I knew things would work out for me," he says.

Ways You Can Get Involved

THERE ARE MANY WAYS YOUNG
PEOPLE CAN MAKE A DIFFERENCE
IN THE LIVES OF HOMELESS PEOPLE.
THE FOLLOWING ARE A FEW SUGGESTIONS
THAT CAN BE APPLIED TO HOMELESS
PEOPLE IN YOUR TOWN OR CITY:

■ Contact a local shelter and ask how you and your friends can be of service in maintaining it. Maybe walls need to be washed or painted, floors need to be scrubbed.

■ Organize your school club or church group to collect canned goods for a local food shelf.

■ Volunteer your services at a shelter as a child-care worker. Many homeless people would like to have time on their own to look for work or more permanent shelter, but those things are far more difficult with little children along.

■ Befriend a homeless child in a shelter. Visit, talk with, take an interest in a person your age. Shelter workers say that getting to know people on a one-to-one basis is the beginning of true understanding.

■ For the next birthday party you give, urge your friends to bring gifts that can be shared with young people in a homeless shelter. Time could even be spent during the party visiting the shelter and bringing the gifts.

■ Places you can write for more information:

Alcoholics Anonymous
General Service Office
P.O. Box 459
Grand Central Station
New York, NY 10163

AA, in understanding the correlation between homelessness and alcoholism, helps individuals battle dependence on alcohol through education and self-help meetings.

National Coalition for the Homeless
1439 Rhode Island Ave. NW
Washington, DC 20005
Offers legislative information for homeless families; also can tell families where nearest shelter is available.

National Low Income Housing Coalition
1012 14th St., NW
Suite 1006
Washington, DC 20005
The coalition lobbies for more and better-quality low-income housing. It also provides educational and organizing services.

Partnership for the Homeless
6 E. 30th St.
New York, NY 10016
This organization provides free meals and medical help for homeless individuals in New York. It also helps families resettle into more permanent housing.

For Further Reading

Judith Berck, *No Place to Be: Voices of Homeless Children*. Boston: Houghton Mifflin, 1992. Highly interesting reading, this book is comprised of stories of homeless children, told in their own words.

Margaret O. Hyde, *The Homeless: Profiling the Problem*. Hillside, NJ: Enslow Publishers, 1989. Excellent section on the medical problems that are worsened by homelessness.

Christopher Jencks, *The Homeless*. Cambridge, MA: Harvard University Press, 1994. Challenging reading, but excellent explanation for the increase in homelessness in the United States in the past five years.

Matthew A. Kraljic, ed., *The Homeless Problem*. New York: H. W. Wilson, 1992. Invaluable, detailed annotated bibliography of pertinent magazine and journal articles about the homeless.

Milton Meltzer, *Poverty in America*. New York: William Morrow, 1986. Helpful chapter on the day-to-day life of urban street people in the 1980s.

Margery G. Nichelason, *Homeless or Hopeless?* Minneapolis: Lerner Publications, 1994. Well written, with excellent photographs, some of them in color.

Karen O'Connor, *Homeless Children*. San Diego: Lucent Books, 1989. Interviews with homeless children make for riveting reading.

Gray Temple, Jr. *Fifty-two Ways to Help Homeless People*. Nashville, TN: Oliver Nelson Publishers, 1991. Informative, easy-reading guide for people wishing to become involved in the lives of homeless people.

Index

alcoholism, 59-60
Trina and, 62-63
Ann
alienation from parents, 48
background of, 36
Arnoldo
career as labor organizer, 82-83
family in Guatemala, 102
first marriage of, 95-96
Guatemalan childhood of, 81
home of, 78-79
life as refugee, 87-88
life on the streets, 93-95, 98-99
personal hygiene of, 80-81
political persecution of, 83-86
religion of, 103-104
trip to United States, 89-90
work in homeless shelter, 92
work of, 100-101

Ben
background of, 36
marine career of, 35
work with police, 37
Ben and Ann
attitudes toward racism, 54-55
becoming homeless, 33-34
difficulty in finding a home, 53
encounter with police, 40-43
reasons for moving to
Minneapolis, 38-39
religion of, 46, 48

black community
drugs and, 39

chemical abuse
as cause of homelessness, 6, 9, 22-23
child abuse
in Marilyn's life, 13, 17-20
Trina and, 60-62
Civil War, 7
crack
as cause of homelessness, 9
financial incentives of, 53
Trina's use of, 64-65

domestic abuse
in Marilyn's life, 17-20
drugs, 38
role in homelessness, 8
education
need for, 53-54

Great Depression, 7

health care costs
as cause of homelessness, 10
HIV diagnosis
of Marilyn and Lisa, 24-25
home school, 15-16
homelessness
causes of, 6, 9, 10
unemployment, 8
number of, 6-7
prevalence of, 6
Housing and Urban
Development, 7

Islam
  adherence to, 40
  tenets of, 46, 48

Lisa (Marilyn's daughter)
  chemical addiction of, 22-24
  children of, 23-24
  diagnosed HIV-positive, 24-25
  sexual abuse of, 20

Marilyn
  abusive relationship with Art, 20-21
  abusive relationships with Emerson, 17-20
  alienation of in school, 16-17
  as victim of child abuse, 13
  becomes homeless, 27-29
  chemical abuse of, 22-23
  childhood of, 11-15
  diagnosed HIV-positive, 24-25
  goals of, 31-32
mentally ill
  number of homeless, 8

National Coalition for the Homeless, 6-7
New Deal, 7

police
  prejudice of, 42
police oppression in

Guatemala, 83
poverty
  as cause of homelessness, 59

racism, 54-55
Robert (Marilyn's grandson)
  violence of, 30
Roosevelt, Franklin D., 7

sexual abuse
  in Marilyn's daughter's life, 20
shelter life, 47-48, 50

tai chi
  Arnoldo's participation in, 103-104
Trina
  abuse of
    by mother, 60-62
  alcoholism of, 62-63
  chemical abuse of
    while pregnant, 73-74
  childhood of, 58-59
  children of, 57
  crack use of, 64-65
  mother of
    alcoholism of, 71-72
    violent behavior, 67-68
  parental alcoholism and, 59-60
  pregnancies of, 63-64

urban renewal
  as cause of homelessness, 9

About the Author

Gail B. Stewart is the author of more than eighty books for children and young adults. She lives in Minneapolis, Minnesota, with her husband Carl and their sons Ted, Eliot, and Flynn. When she is not writing, she spends her time reading, walking, and watching her sons play soccer.

Although she has enjoyed working on each of her books, she says that *The Other America* series has been especially gratifying. "So many of my past books have involved extensive research," she says, "but most of it has been library work—journals, magazines, books. But for these books, the main research has been very human. Spending the day with a little girl who has AIDS, or having lunch in a soup kitchen with a homeless man—these kinds of things give you insight that a library alone just can't match."

Stewart hopes that readers of this series will experience some of the same insights—perhaps even being motivated to use some of the suggestions at the end of each book to become involved with someone of the Other America.

About the Photographer

Mark Ahlstrom has worked in publishing for over twenty years, producing over two hundred books for young adults.